Wicked
NEW HAMPSHIRE

Wicked
New Hampshire

Renee Mallett

THE
History
PRESS

Published by The History Press
Charleston, SC
www.historypress.com

First published 2020

Manufactured in the United States

ISBN 9781467144155

Library of Congress Control Number: 2020934442

Notice: The information in this book is true and complete to the best of our knowledge. It is offered without guarantee on the part of the author or The History Press. The author and The History Press disclaim all liability in connection with the use of this book.

Wickedness is a myth invented by good people
to account for the curious attractiveness of others.

—*Oscar Wilde*

CONTENTS

CONTENTS

PREFACE

*I*nside these pages you'll find some odd, scandalous and remarkable true tales from New Hampshire's storied history—enjoy! One of the lovely things about the New England states is how many of our historic places are protected and still standing. If you're moved to explore some of the places that you read about in this book, I encourage it wholeheartedly. Many of the people you're about to learn about moved around in spaces that still exist to this day. In many towns, you'll find all kinds of guided history walks that will show you around notable places in New Hampshire. But please keep in mind that not all of these places are open for tours. Many historic homes are, to this day, just that—someone's home. Please ask before exploring and use your best judgment about what places are open to the public and which are not.

Your local historical society is a valuable resource if you're looking for some wicked history in your own town. New Hampshire has long been home to a quirky cast of eccentrics, and it seems like every city and town in the Granite State has a few wicked tales in its past.

INTRODUCTION

*E*ach year I take time out of my hectic family life with five kids to visit Star Island, New Hampshire, for a silent meditation retreat. I can't say how well I do on the silent part of the trip, but I love the time I spend with an amazing group of people in such a unique place. Star Island is gorgeous. Even as the second-largest island in the grouping that makes up the Isles of Shoals, it's small—just forty-six acres—a windswept, rocky ledge butting up to the gentle cold blue caress of the Atlantic. The Unitarians own it now, along with the Oceanic Hotel, which has been on the island in one form or another since 1873, and they use it to host a series of summer retreats—watercolor painting, meditation, writing, yoga and more. Despite its religious affiliation, everyone is welcome on Star Island, regardless of their religion or lack thereof. But even for the atheists, there's something spiritual at work in this curious place. Talk to a Star Island enthusiast, and you'll hear a lot of the same words again and again: peace, tranquility, power, energy. For many people, there is an undeniable pull to this little jumble of rocks just nine miles southeast of the mouth of the Piscataqua River. While it feels like the remote ends of the earth, it's a mere twelve miles from the dock of the Isles of Shoals Steamship Company to the middle of Gosport Harbor.

This peaceful little escape belies its strange history. Originally settled by fishermen and tax dodgers, the Isles of Shoals, Star Island included, welcomed pirates long before Unitarians. The past of the Isles of Shoals is filled with murders, buried treasure and even legends of vampires.

But in a way, that makes it the most New Hampshire place in all of New Hampshire. Though the forty-sixth smallest state, New Hampshire was the first of the original thirteen colonies to adopt its own constitution. It is rife with stunning natural landscapes, quaint little towns and a "Live Free or Die" attitude that sometimes results in a darker and more scandalous past than many would imagine.

I've been writing about New Hampshire for more than fifteen years now. I've called the Granite State my home even longer. In books like *Manchester Ghosts* and *Ghosts of Portsmouth, New Hampshire*, among others, I've gotten to explore the supernatural side of the state I call home. Oftentimes in my research for those books, I have come across perfectly true bits of history and odd places around the state that are far stranger than a few ghosts could ever be.

I'm actually writing this from the wide front porch of the Oceanic Hotel on Star Island. I have a usual corner where I set up shop with my pen and notepad or sketchbook and pencil or a tangle of yarn waiting to be turned into a sweater, depending on whatever project catches my attention at any given moment. The sun is shining, but I have a hoodie pulled up over my head because there is a touch of fall in the air already. Yesterday, boats to and from the mainland were canceled because of the size of the waves. A few swallows dart quickly through the air, nearly at eye level because of the way the Oceanic perches up on the rocks overlooking Gosport Harbor. Seagulls circle around the edges of the masses of these smaller birds. The gulls are predatory and four times their size, like great white sharks of the sky. Last year, when it was ninety degrees all week and the air was thick with swallows, I saw a gull swoop out of nowhere to snatch one of the fledglings out of the sky mid-flight.

Fifteen feet below my usual spot rocking on the porch, three boys play baseball on the front lawn, probably the closest thing there is to a flat space on Star. Because there are only three of them, they take on multiple roles in the game, a feat that even they can't keep track of. As they play, it sounds like that old comedy bit, "Who's on first? Where is third?" Though they can't keep their teams or places straight, they seem to be having the time of their lives. The face of one boy in particular, wearing what another generation would have called Coke bottle glasses, is alight with the kind of joy usually reserved for Christmas mornings.

"I'm doing it," he yells triumphantly. "I'm really doing it!"

Soon after, when a super slow ball rolls between his feet uncaught, he swipes at the glasses and reminds his friends, "I never did this before. My depth perception is not the greatest."

A 1902 postcard showing the dock at Star Island looking very much the same as the dock that stands there today. *Library of Congress public domain.*

Past their heads, beyond the four or so boats dotting Gosport Harbor, is the even smaller and more desolate expanse of Smuttynose Island. A man-made breakwater connects Star and Smuttynose, and even an average swimmer would have no trouble swimming between the two islands, but Smuttynose belongs to the state of Maine, and Star Island is considered part of New Hampshire. The two states have split the islands that make up the Isles of Shoals, though not always peacefully. Bickering over the islands and the state line that splits them has made it all the way to the Supreme Court. But intangible state lines mean nothing to the shoals—and mean even less when it comes to wickedness. Smuttynose, with its grand total of two buildings and a single flagpole, was once the site of a grim murder that would later be immortalized in Anita Shreve's *The Weight of Water*.

But that was in 1873. Today it's 2019, and the sun is shining despite the cool breeze. A boat from the mainland, the *Thomas Leighton*, is approaching the pier, ready to discharge its load of passengers, who come twice daily in the summer to marvel at this little slice of New Hampshire history that is as frozen in time as any other place they'll probably ever visit. Some of them, though increasingly fewer each year, might ask a Pelican (as the staff have been affectionately called since the inception of the hotel) about the

Smuttynose murders or about their chances of finding Blackbeard's lost treasure. Many more will ask about the island's solar panel array, the largest off-grid one in the state, located behind the hotel. This, I guess, is what people mean when they talk about progress.

There is a meaty *thwack*, and one of the ball players yells out, "I think we should stop; you keep getting hit in the face." But his friend just laughs and begs them to keep on playing.

Above my head, the wind, perhaps the one constant thing on Star Island, snaps two flags, one rainbow striped for Pride and the other bright pink on white for the Unitarians Universalist. The pier stretching out to Gosport Harbor is now alive with tourists. Those who have never been to the island before and don't know how different the weather can be from Portsmouth's look cold. I can't think of a single spot, indoors or outside, where they won't see a stunning ocean view. But if they spend too long marveling at the waves and not looking down at their feet, they are likely to trip over some forgotten bit of history working its way up through the shallow topsoil. It could be good history or it could be bad—the same as you might find anywhere else in the Granite State.

—Renee Mallett
Oceanic Hotel, Star Island
2019

1

H.H. HOLMES,
AMERICA'S FIRST SERIAL KILLER

With the plentitude of books and movies that have been created and continue to come out about madmen like Charles Manson, John Wayne Gacy and Jeffrey Dahmer, many people think that the public's fascination with serial killers is a solely modern invention. This is not so. The American public has always feasted on the darker side of human experience, and the interest in H.H. Holmes proves the point.

Long before he was credited as America's first serial killer and called H.H. Holmes, he was Herman Webster Mudgett. Mudgett was born on May 16, 1861, in Gilmanton, New Hampshire, to Levi and Theodate Mudgett. His parents have been described as devout Methodists. From a young age, the boy showed a keen intelligence and an interest in medicine, although that interest seemed as though it came by way of a traumatic childhood incident. Young Herman Mudgett, as notable for his small stature as he was for his brains, had a long-running fear of Gilmanton's family doctor. Schoolhouse rumors persisted that this kindly old small-town doctor kept a collection of human heads and amputated limbs tucked away inside a large cabinet in his office. When Mudgett was five or six years old, a gang of older boys, knowing his fear, dragged him into the office to scare him. They didn't find any human heads, but Mudgett started to shriek wildly when he saw the anatomical skeleton in the corner of the doctor's office. This only spurred on the cruel prank. The older boys dragged the younger one over and tried to force him to touch the skeleton. Finally hearing the commotion, the doctor rushed in and saved the boy. From this time on, Mudgett expressed his interest in medicine and begin experimenting on animals. He claimed to be learning anatomy, but his true interest was seeing how long he could operate on an animal while it was still alive.

At the age of sixteen, Herman married Clara Lovering. He fathered a son, Robert Lovering Mudgett, with her two years later. During this time, he apprenticed under Dr. Nahum Wight, a New Hampshire doctor who lived in Gilmanton but had found an odd sort of fame as an outspoken advocate for human dissection. But even with this cover for his medical experiments, Mudgett was restless. New Hampshire couldn't seem to hold him. He moved the young family to Burlington, Vermont, so he could attend university there. Within a year, he'd move them again, this time to the University of Michigan so he could begin his training as a surgeon. Despite his clear intelligence, Mudgett was only a so-so student. This may have been because he was busy with other schemes. In later years, he would admit to using cadavers stolen from the medical school to defraud insurance companies during this period of his life. At one point, he was almost prevented from graduating when a wealthy widowed hairdresser showed up on campus to complain that Mudgett had promised to marry her and walked off with some of her jewelry and money. But Mudgett explained that it must be a case of mistaken identity. He, of course, was already married. The scandal soon blew over, and things continued on their course for Herman. Soon, Mr. Mudgett became Dr. Mudgett.

From the outside, everything seemed to be going well for the newly minted doctor. But his irrepressible dark side was coming closer and closer to the surface. His wife, Clara, fled back to her family in Alton, New Hampshire, to get away from his violent and abusive ways. Around this time, in Philadelphia, the first documented killing involving Dr. Mudgett occured, although some believe his true first victim was a boy in New Hampshire who fell to his death while the two children were exploring an abandoned house. At the time, it was believed that this was really an accident, and to this day he has not been confirmed as one of Mudgett's victims. The first person known to have died by Mudgett's hands was in Philadelphia. Mudgett had moved to the city to work as a pharmacist after medical school. Despite his advanced education, a customer died when given the incorrect medication. Even now it is unclear if this was the first clumsy murder of a serial killer or a mistake that may have opened the door to the dark passenger that had long been simmering below Dr. Mudgett's surface.

Mudgett, now calling himself Dr. Holmes to distance himself from the dead patient in Philadelphia, arrived in Chicago in 1886. He hoped that the change in name and the hundreds of miles he'd put between himself and the Philadelphia death would grant him a lease on a new life. He had cut all ties with his family in Gilmanton, but if they had heard of the move, they wouldn't have been surprised. As an eleven-year-old boy, he'd developed a fascination with the city of Chicago when he heard the news of its destruction. During the Great Fire of Chicago in October 1871, more than 2,112 acres of prime downtown real estate had been destroyed. But like Holmes himself, Chicago was a phoenix rising from the ashes. It was only fifteen years since Mrs. O'Leary's cow had been scapegoated for the destruction of seventeen thousand buildings, but now, with the help of twenty-nine countries contributing aid and even New Hampshire's own Amoskeag Manufacturing Company gifting new fire engines, the city had been rebuilt many times over—bigger and more modern than before.

In Englewood, Mudgett would have the chance to catch a bit of Chicago's shooting star. On Sixty-Third Street, he found employment, once again, as a druggist. His employer did not, it seems, look too hard at either his name or his experience. And truly, she had no reason to. Dr. Holmes quickly showed his skill at the job, not just in blending together medications for whatever ailed one but also by charming every customer who walked through the door. Holmes had an outgoing, flirty personality that served him well with customers, especially the young female ones.

Holmes was doing so well at the pharmacy that he even offered to buy it from the current owner, a widowed woman who was finding it increasingly difficult to run the store, even with the help of handsome Dr. Holmes. She gladly accepted the offer. But sadly, things took a quick turn for the worse as soon as the arrangements were made. Dr. Holmes never came through with the purchase price, and the two fought viciously over the store. Things became bad enough that legal action was taken against Dr. Holmes for nonpayment. But the case would never go to court. Shortly after the court case was filed, Dr. Holmes's former employer disappeared and was never heard from again.

This freed up Holmes, and his bank account, to take the next step in creating his empire. He quickly bought the property across the street from the pharmacy and started construction of a remarkable, for the time, building. Three stories high, it featured shops along the street level and a collection of rooms and apartments, said to number in the hundreds, on the floors above.

Fascinated neighbors quickly dubbed the building, which covered an entire city block, the "Castle."

Part of the neighborhood's interest was sparked by just how long it took to build the Castle. What should have been several months of work for a crew of skilled craftsmen instead took years. The problem was that every few weeks Dr. Holmes would fire the crew and hire all new laborers. Part of this was done to cheat the workers out of their wages. At the time, carpenters would work for several weeks before expecting to be paid. Holmes could fire them for one trumped-up offense or another and refuse payment for all of the work they'd already completed. But the real motive was so that no one person, other than Dr. Holmes, who designed the building himself, would have a clear idea of how it all went together. The reason for the deception would only be clear many years later when police discovered the Castle was actually a house of horrors. While some of the rooms were normal, others featured hidden gas pipes ready to smother visitors while they slept with the simple flip of a switch. Stairs led several flights up or down just to end at bricked-over walls. Doors opened to nothing. A hidden walk-in bank vault adjacent to Dr. Holmes's office was made totally airtight so victims would slowly smother to death inside. A vat of acid bubbled away in the basement next to a surgical table. An eight-foot-tall oven, large enough to hold an entire man, sat in Dr. Holmes's personal office. Along with the secret passageways and deathly obstacles, a greased shaft ran through the center of the building to the basement surgical room, where Holmes would clean and bleach bodies before sending the skeletons off to be sold as medical specimens to colleges and doctors.

Trapdoors and false walls littered the structure, all the better to confuse any victims who might somehow slip away from Dr. Holmes—and victims there were. In an incredible stroke of luck (good for Holmes and bad for his victims), the Castle was finished just in time to start accepting boarders who were flooding Chicago to visit the World's Fair. Built to celebrate the 400th anniversary of Columbus discovering the New World, the city of Chicago created a stunning white city filled with every wonder of the day. It drew 751,026 visitors on its opening day alone. Ultimately, an estimated 27.5 million visitors would walk the canal-lined fairway, many of them visiting Chicago from around the country and around the globe for the very first time. It was an incredible boon to the city and its residents. Any Chicago resident with a spare room to rent made a mint during the run of the World's Fair. And right there in Englewood was the respectable Dr. Holmes, who had one hundred rooms to rent. While neighbors may have called his building the Castle, Dr. Holmes called it the World's Fair Hotel. He began advertising for tenants with the promise of a cheap room to stay in while visiting the attraction.

We know that Dr. Holmes visited the fair at least twice himself, accompanied by Annie and Minnie Williams, sisters who would fall victim to the serial killer after enjoying the spectacle of the fair. They are just two among an untold number of people who went to Chicago to enjoy the fair and ended up being dissected in Dr. Holmes's basement laboratory. Many of the corpses would be cleaned of their flesh and their skeletons articulated for sale. Dr. Holmes made $200 a victim in this way alone.

Along the way, Dr. Holmes also married three women, though he never divorced his first wife, Clara Lovering, who was still patiently back home in New Hampshire raising his son. Many of the wives, and the estimated 150 stenographers and secretaries he employed over his few years in Chicago, signed over any property or money they had to Dr. Holmes. As with the former employer who had caused him trouble, many were never heard from again.

Ultimately, it wasn't murder, polygamy or even missing secretaries that knocked over the first domino and alerted law enforcement to Dr. Holmes's wicked ways. It was simple insurance fraud. Even with his murder castle rented nightly and pockets full of money stolen from women who fell for his smooth-talking ways, Dr. Holmes could never seem to give up on the insurance fraud schemes he had used to pay his way through medical school. Dr. Holmes called on his longtime partner in crime, Benjamin Pitezel, and asked for his help in the con. A $10,000 life insurance policy was bought for Pitezel, and the pair headed for Philadelphia to fake Pitezel's death. Pitezel probably knew about at least some of the people Holmes had killed over the years, but he never imagined that his longtime employer would murder him. But in a complicated, convoluted plot, Dr. Holmes ended up killing his longtime associate and then assisting the insurance company in investigating the death.

Finally, Dr. Holmes had overplayed his hand. The scene of the death, even with the very real body of Benjamin Pitezel and not a stand-in corpse stolen from a medical school, was clearly staged. It did not take long for the insurance company to start to question what had really happened to Benjamin Pitezel in Philadelphia.

With an insurance investigator hot on his trail, Dr. Holmes began a bizarre state-crossing adventure. When speaking with Pitezel's widow, who had an inkling of what her husband's work with Dr. Holmes had really entailed, the brazen Dr. Holmes managed to convince her that Pitezel was still alive and waiting for her to meet him in Canada. Holmes was worried that the widow, or even some of the couple's children, might have enough information to help insurance investigators uncover the true depths of his crime. He was able to talk the widow into letting him take three of her young children with him while sending her on a cross-country trip to meet up with Pitezel. At the same time as Dr. Holmes was slowly moving the widow Pitezel north, along with the gaggle of three children under his care, he was also maneuvering his recently wed bride around the country, sometimes having all of this trusting cast of characters staying, unbeknownst to them, in hotels just blocks away from one another. He'd spend the night with his newlywed bride, meet the widow for breakfast with a forged note from her husband and then sneak off for an hour or two to take the Pitezel children to the zoo—all without raising suspicion. Whatever else can be said of H.H. Holmes, the man surely knew how to multitask.

Just before his arrest by the Boston Police, Dr. Holmes returned to New Hampshire to visit the family left behind. After being estranged from his parents for years, Holmes returned to his boyhood home in Gilmanton. He even stopped in Tilton to spend an afternoon with Clara and their son, Robert. Most amazingly of all, while visiting Clara, he admitted to marrying another woman while still married to her. But the tale he spun to excuse his behavior was as outrageous as any other tale he ever told. Holmes told Clara that he had been in a terrible train wreck, resulting in a long hospital stay and amnesia. During that time, he fell in love with a patroness of the hospital and married her, having no recollection of his true first marriage to Clara. But, claimed Holmes, he had recently been the recipient of an advanced brain surgery that brought back all of his memories. Amazingly, by all accounts, Clara believed this tall tale.

Back in Boston, the police, the insurance investigators and the Pinkertons were all closing in. Dr. Holmes must have had more than a sneaking suspicion that they were about to catch up to him. After returning from his New Hampshire sojourn, Dr. Holmes began contacting steamship companies, looking to book passage to Europe for himself and his latest wife. Seeing their suspect heading in and out of the booking companies, the police decided they could wait no longer. Four were dispatched to arrest the doctor, who went quietly. Once Dr. Holmes was safely in jail, the investigations had a chance to continue. The police felt sure that they had enough evidence of insurance fraud to put the doctor away, but there were enough rumors and odd remarks to convince them that Dr. Holmes may have been guilty of much worse crimes. Very quickly, more and more of these crimes came to light. As word spread that Dr. Holmes was being looked at by the police, more people came forward. Dr. Holmes was sued by several people and businesses that he had defrauded over the years. More than fifty people brought charges against him in Englewood alone. Police from Texas showed up with an arrest warrant for horse theft.

Even the Chicago Gas Company that serviced the Castle had a nefarious story to share about Dr. Holmes. Years prior, it had discovered him trying to swindle investors by pretending to have invented a machine that turned water into a sort of electricity. He led the group to one room of his basement lair, turned a tap and showed them the strange illumination he created, he said, with simple tap water. Really, the strange contraption hid an illegal link to the city gas line. The gas company had gotten wind of the swindle and cut the line shortly after. They could not explain why criminal charges had never been filed.

But the very worst of his crimes had yet to be fully uncovered. The widow Pitezel was working closely with police trying to locate her three missing children, taken by Dr. Holmes. A grand jury in Philadelphia would indict him on charges of insurance fraud even as investigators crisscrossed the country frantically looking for the three children.

Along the way, they talked to all of Dr. Holmes's remaining wives and tracked down any number of frauds and failed schemes. At this point, the case of Dr. Holmes became a media sensation, rivaling that of any other seen before. At first, the reports were almost flattering, marveling at his audacious schemes and good looks. Newspapers described him as a debonair, brazen criminal, a true man of his times who was just trying to amass wealth and travel the world by any means possible. One paper declared him "the arch conspirator." The *Chicago Tribune* proclaimed that he was the "smoothest and best all-around swindle" the city had ever seen. It was not until more stories broke about the piles of bones found in the basement of the murder Castle and the bodies of the three missing children, burned and buried in various spots around the country, that the public turned on Holmes.

Dr. Holmes himself gave three confessions while in prison, variously claiming to have killed more than two hundred people to saying he was innocent of all charges. Sometimes Holmes claimed that he had never killed anyone, but he had seen a mysterious Mr. Hatch, of whom no trace would ever be found, kill all of the people credited as his own victims. Sometimes Dr. Holmes confessed to murdering people who would then turn up very much alive. In one instance, he proclaimed that one of his victims, one of the Williams sisters who had accompanied him to the World's Fair, had killed

WAGES OF HIS SIN.

Herman Webster Mudgett, alias H. H. Holmes, Arch-Fiend and Multi-Murderer, Pays the Penalty for His Crime on the Gallows Yesterday.

Confessed Murderer of Twenty-Seven People, Convicted of the Murder of One, and Known to Have Killed Many, Hanged at Philadelphia.

DIED AFTER ASSERTING HIS INNOCENCE.

Before the Black Cap Shut Out the World he Denied Guilt of Pitezel's Murder—His Statement on the Gallows Before the Drop.

The Stoical Character of the Fiend Never Yielded—Received Religious Consolation up to the Hour of Death —Holmes' Career.

From the collection of the author.

her sister. Holmes claimed he was guilty of nothing more than trying to help her cover up the crime.

With each confession, printed full bore in newspapers, there would quickly come a retraction from Dr. Holmes, whom the papers now declared "an arch-fiend" whose good looks hid the face of a monster. Dr. Holmes would even write and publish a book about his own life while sitting in jail, trying to cash in on the public's fascination with him. He showed a remarkable flair for marketing.

Ultimately, after a six-day trial that many of the time compared to that of Lizzie Borden's, Dr. Holmes was found guilty of one murder, that of

Benjamin Pitezel, done to secure a body to commit insurance fraud. Within three weeks, the Pennsylvania Supreme Court had turned down his motions for appeal. Dr. Holmes was sentenced to hang for the murder he had been convicted of, even as investigators tracked down more evidence of his other crimes. But Holmes was not done in the limelight. In one final grab for attention, he published yet another confession, stating, "I was born with the devil in me. I could not help the fact that I was a murderer, no more than the poet can help the inspiration to sing—I was born with the 'Evil One' standing as my sponsor beside the bed where I was ushered into the world, and he has been with me since."

In this final confession, sold to the Hearst Corporation for $10,000, Holmes admitted to twenty-seven murders and any number of fraud and schemes. He said he had intended to murder Pitezel's widow and all of the Pitezel children, instead of just the three he had killed on his cross country trip. Despite the fact that the widow and two of the children survived, Dr. H.H. Holmes felt that he should get credit for those as well.

On May 7, 1896, Dr. Holmes was led to the gallows and hanged until he was dead. It was nine days short of his thirty-fifth birthday. With his last words, he offered one final retraction of all of his confessions. As the hangman's noose swung in front of him, Holmes claimed to have killed just two women. By all accounts, the murderer then sharpened the crease on his pants and slid his head into the noose. It would take fifteen minutes for him to die. In a final bit of irony, the killer, who had violated so many corpses and sold off so many skeletons, was buried in a coffin filled and sealed with layers of cement. Holmes, it seems, was terrified of his body being treated the same way he had treated so many others.

His famed murder Castle would fare no better than the man who had designed it. After the investigation was complete, a police officer reopened the three-story structure as a murder museum and charged visitors fifteen cents to wander the labyrinthine hallways and peek into the oddly shaped rooms where an untold number of people had died. But just two weeks after the venture started, it went up in smoke—literally. In the middle of the night, the Castle burned to the ground. No cause was ever found, though police suspected arson.

Back home in Tilton, New Hampshire, Clara Lovering Mudgett refused all inquiries from the press. Soon she would remarry and become Clara Lovering Peverly. She lived a quiet life and died at the age of ninety-five. Her grave can be found in Maple Grove Cemetery in Canterbury, New Hampshire.

2

LUCY LAMBERT HALE

*I*f you think Clara Lovering had a tough go of it when it came to marriage, consider the case of poor Lucy Lambert Hale. Born in Dover, New Hampshire, in 1841, she was the second-oldest daughter of New Hampshire senator and famed abolitionist John Parker Hale. Even at a young age, her beauty was notable. By the tender age of twelve, she already had a wildly inappropriate suitor, a Harvard University student named William Chandler who sent her love letters and poems by post regularly.

Senator Hale had some concerns about his daughter's sway over men. Around the time the letters started arriving from college boys, he sent Lucy to a prim and proper boarding school in Hanover—girls only, no boys allowed. One of her suitors, a Harvard sophomore who would go on to spend thirty years as an associate justice in the U.S. Supreme Court, sent young Lucy Hale letters joking that the boarding school was a nunnery because its purpose was to keep her chaste.

If there was one man who the young Lucy was connected to that her father did approve of, it was Robert Todd Lincoln. While on vacation as a child, the oldest son of future president Abraham Lincoln struck up a close friendship with Lucy that her father did everything in his power to turn into something more. His efforts to betroth the two were no secret. But time after time, Senator Hale failed to create an engagement between Lucy and the young Mr. Lincoln.

Left: Lucy Lambert Hale was considered a great beauty in her day. *Library of Congress public domain.*

Right: Lucy Hale's father, a senator from New Hampshire, hoped to make a match between his daughter and Robert Todd Lincoln (pictured above). *Library of Congress public domain.*

Lucy Lambert Hale came of age in Washington, D.C., where she was noted for her beauty and flirtatious manner, during the Civil War. While she spent her days volunteering for the Sanitation Committee, a kind of early precursor to the Red Cross, she was a usual fixture at the parties and balls that went on all evening long. One contemporary article described the senator's daughter's personality as "a subtle brew of flattery, teasing, and cajoling."

It was while living in D.C. on Valentine's Day in 1862 that the vivacious Miss Hale received an unusual bit of correspondence:

> *My Dear Miss Hale*
> *Were it not for the License which a time-honored observance of this day allows, I had not written you this poor note....You resemble in a most remarkable degree a lady, very dear to me, now dead and your close resemblance to her surprised me the first time I saw you. This must be my apology for any apparent rudeness noticeable.—To see you has indeed*

afforded me a melancholy pleasure, if you can conceive of such, and should
we never meet nor I see you again—believe me, I shall always associate you
in my memory, with her, who was very beautiful, and whose face, like your
own I trust, was a faithful index of gentleness and amiability.
With a Thousand kind wishes for your future happiness I am, to you—
A Stranger

In short time, Lucy would discover the name of the mysterious stranger who sent her such compliments. The stranger, as it turned out, was someone who was really no stranger all. Most cultured people of the day knew the name of this stranger, even if they had never had the chance to meet him in person. The writer was none other than John Wilkes Booth. Booth, then twenty-four, was the heartthrob of his day. An accomplished actor, described in the press as outrageously handsome, he was said to possess the manner of a true southern gentleman. It should probably go without saying that Booth was popular with the ladies.

Booth had just finished a nationwide tour as Romeo, making as many headlines when a jealous actress tried to stab him with a dagger before attempting to take her own life as he did for his acting chops. She might have been toying with men's hearts since her teens, but Miss Lucy Hale was as smitten as any other young woman would be when pursued by a handsome, famous actor who sent her secret admirer letters. Miss Hale had finally met her romantic match.

Or, perhaps, it was Booth who had met his match. While Booth was long considered a roguish ladies' man, by all accounts, he seemed as genuinely taken with Lucy Hale as she was with him. They were seen regularly galivanting around town, and by March 1865, the couple was secretly engaged—well, sort of secretly. It seems that John Wilkes Booth told his family about the engagement. It was Lucy Hale's family who were kept in the dark. Part of the need for secrecy was simple class judgement of the time. Booth might be famous, but that didn't make him good enough to marry a senator's daughter. And there was the pesky problem that Senator Hale still held out hope of marrying his daughter off to Robert Todd Lincoln.

Robert Lincoln would become something of a sore spot for John Wilkes Booth. It is said that he was insanely jealous of the president's son. Booth quarreled many times with Lucy over the time she spent with her old friend. Real sparks flew when Washington, D.C. newspapers reported that Lucy spent the night dancing with Lincoln in the ballroom of the National Hotel.

John Wilkes Booth was a popular actor in his day but was wildly jealous of Lucy Hale's friends and suitors. *Library of Congress public domain.*

All of this was further complicated by the fact that John Wilkes Booth was, at the same time, in a series of complicated plots to kidnap Robert's father, President Abraham Lincoln. The kidnapping plans failed several times, but that didn't deter John Wilkes Booth from hatching an even more grandiose plan. Unknown to Lucy, her secret fiancée was now planning to assassinate the father of her childhood friend.

John Wilkes Booth attended the second inauguration of President Abraham Lincoln. He went with a ticket that was given to him by none other than Lucy Lambert Hale. Even by April 14, the day of the assassination, Lucy was still in the dark that her fiance was planning to kill the father of one of her oldest friends—a friend her father still tried to maneuver into becoming her husband. Lucy spent the afternoon of the assassination learning Spanish, practicing for an upcoming trip. President Lincoln had just named Senator Hale ambassador to Spain, and Lucy was counting on going there with him.

This is not to say that Lucy had no idea her fiance hated President Lincoln. John Wilkes Booth was on record as being a fierce supporter of slavery. Booth believed so strongly in the case for slavery that he even belonged to a Richmond, Virginia militia that was on hand for the hanging of abolitionist John Brown. (As Lucy was the daughter of an equally vigorous advocate against slavery, this must have caused some rousing conversation between her and Booth.) Booth, it should be noted, was known to be quick to fly off the handle. Even at a young age, his emotional instability was notable. It only became worse as he got older, and his fits of jealousy were nearly legendary.

Lucy Lambert Hale would never marry John Wilkes Booth. Booth shot President Lincoln at Ford's Theater the night of April 14 and was shot down himself near Port Royal, Virginia, twelve days later. In possession of the assassin when he died was a portrait of Lucy Hale—and those of four other women, all actresses. Even while Lucy tried to come to terms with the fact that her secret fiance was a murderer, Senator Hale went on the defensive. Immediately following the death of Booth, Senator Hale met privately with President Andrew Johnson. No one knows what Hale might have said to explain away his daughter's relationship with the president killer, but whatever it was satisfied Johnson. Senator Hale convinced the new president to do everything he could to keep his daughter's name out of the government's investigation into the assassination. Legal matters secured in his favor, Hale next had to sway the public's opinion about his daughter's involvement in the events of April 14, 1865. He wrote one letter after another for publication in any paper that would print it, denying Lucy's romantic connection with Booth, no matter what photos he might have had on his person when he shot Lincoln.

Lucy Lambert Hale escaped the scandal soundly. She was never called to share with investigators anything she may have known about Booth and his plot. She was free to accompany her father on his ambassadorship in Spain. She would become the toast of Europe. Many aristocrats from many countries made their play for the flirtatious American, but perhaps remembering how her last engagement had gone, she turned down every offer of marriage that came her way.

Miss Hale returned to New Hampshire in 1870, when her father's health started to fail. Four years later, she finally got married. The man who captured her heart was the same Harvard University student who had tried wooing her when she was twelve years old. William Chandler had become a lawyer after Harvard and now occupied a position that Lucy was very familiar with—U.S. senator of New Hampshire. Together they lived a life full of politics and parties, until Lucy's death on October 15, 1915. She is buried at Pine Hill Cemetery in Dover, New Hampshire.

3

GOVERNOR WENTWORTH'S WEDDING

efore you start thinking that only New Hampshire women make some odd choices in life partners, let's stop for a moment and consider the case of Governor Benning Wentworth. The Portsmouth native and Harvard alum became governor of the Province of New Hampshire in 1741, after being instrumental in making the case that the British colony deserved its own overseer instead of being administered by the neighboring Massachusetts Bay Colony.

While Benning Wentworth was a well-known and quite prosperous merchant in Portsmouth, his true wealth came from politics. His dual roles as governor and king's surveyor general put him in a unique position. Wentworth was able to fill his pockets by selling off land grants in what is now Vermont. The Province of New York felt it had jurisdiction over many of these land grants, and the entire enterprise was controversial. The legal battle over these land grants would last well past Benning's term as governor and wouldn't be settled until Vermont was declared its own state.

The real matter that earns Governor Wentworth his place in the shocking annals of New Hampshire history is his choice of wife. His first wife was Abigail Ruck and was a pretty standard match for his time period. But Abigail Ruck died in 1755 when Benning was just fifty-nine. It was his choice in his second wife that sparked gossip among his Portsmouth neighbors. In 1760, at the age of sixty-four, Benning planned a lavish dinner party and invited a who's who of Portsmouth elite. Little did any of them realize that the dinner party was actually an impromptu wedding.

The Wentworth-Coolidge Museum in Portsmouth was once the house where Governor Wentworth married his much younger maid during a dinner party. *Photo used with permission from the Portsmouth Athenaeum.*

Governor Benning, in a surprise move, married his twenty-three-year-old maid, Martha Hilton, in his dining room while his surprised guests looked on. The marriage was shocking for several reasons. Not only was Martha more than forty years his junior and a maid, but she had been all but raised by the Wentworth family and was actually a servant during the latter years of Abigail Ruck's life.

Riddled with gout, Governor Wentworth was an unpleasant man with an unpleasant face and a body to match his demeanor. Rumors said that Martha Hilton, looking even younger than her twenty-three years, appeared in front of the oversized fireplace in the dining room of the forty-room Wentworth-Coolidge mansion in a silk dress for the surprise wedding. Later descendants of the governor would dispute these accounts, claiming Miss Hilton was thirty-three at the time of her wedding and that she wore calico, as if the fabric of the dress was what was causing the consternation and not the station and age of the bride.

It was not just the upper crust of Portsmouth elite who were shocked by the pairing. Stories survive of servants refusing to take orders from the newly minted Mrs. Wentworth because of her former position among them.

The role of Governor Wentworth, and his unusual marriage, can't be overstated. Both Bennington, Vermont, and Bennington, New Hampshire, are named for the salacious politician. Henry Wadsworth Longfellow's famous poem "Lady Wentworth" is based on the rags-to-riches marriage.

Martha Hilton Wentworth would have the last laugh over her neighbors' wagging tongues. She outlived Governor Wentworth by a number of years and was the sole heir to the enormous fortune he had amassed selling Vermont land grants. She remarried soon after Benning's death, this time to her late husband's cousin Michael Wentworth.

4

JUDGE JOHN PICKERING

New Hampshire holds the dubious distinction of being the state with the first impeached federal judge. But John Pickering's early life never would have made anyone suspect that impeachment would be the thing he would become known for so long after his death. Pickering was born in Newington, New Hampshire, on September 22, 1737. From an early age, Pickering showed an affinity to religion that bordered on zealotry, but the life of a preacher never would have suited him. As a young man, John Pickering turned down a position in the clergy, believing he could do more good working in the field of law. That Judge Pickering was intelligent enough to do good as a lawyer was indisputable. When he graduated from Harvard in 1761, it was said that he spoke more than twenty different languages. Pickering made his name as a lawyer, soon moving his offices from Greenland to Portsmouth as his reputation grew.

His move from the law to politics came in 1783, when he was first elected to the New Hampshire State Legislature. Five years later, he was selected to represent the state in the first Constitutional Congress in Philadelphia. This occasion marked the first time that it became public knowledge that something might be a little off about John Pickering. He turned down his spot in the Philadelphia Constitutional Congress because he was both a wild hypochondriac and absolutely terrified of crossing water.

From 1790 to 1795, Pickering served as the chief justice of what was then called the New Hampshire Superior Court of Judicature. Judge Pickering's time on the bench there was marked by spells from a strange illness—namely outrageous drinking binges and soul-crushing hangovers. His attendance and performance were so bad that some tried to get him removed from the bench.

As an alternative solution, no less than George Washington himself tried to help Pickering save face by appointing him to the U.S. District Court for the District of New Hampshire. This served a dual purpose. Pickering would not have the shame of being removed but would instead be moved up to a court that saw few actual cases. At best, the lessened workload would give him the time and space to work out his problems. At worst, his poor behavior would impact fewer people.

Judge John Pickering graduated from Harvard and spoke several languages, but his time on the bench was marred by scandal. *Library of Congress public domain.*

Unfortunately, Judge Pickering did not make good use of the extra time the promotion afforded him. By 1800, it was more common for him to not appear in court than it was for him to show up and do the work. Many of the court records from this time reflect his poor attendance. Even today, there are numerous copies noted, "The court was adjourned, due to absence of judge." Worse than Pickering not showing up was his behavior when he did. Often, he would fall asleep, which sounds terrible, until one considers that when he wasn't sleeping, lawyers had to handle him swearing, ranting and raving.

A court clerk, fed up and at the end of his rope, wrote asking for a replacement judge on April 25, 1801, calling Judge Pickering deranged. There was enough evidence to support this conclusion for Judge Pickering to be granted a short break and for Jeremiah Smith to be named his temporary replacement. All was well for a short period of time in the U.S. District Court for the District of New Hampshire. Then Judge Pickering returned, none the better for his sabbatical.

Things went on, more or less as they had been all along, until November 1802, when Pickering was tasked with hearing the case *United States vs. The Eliza*. The case would prove to be the last straw for Judge Pickering. The *Eliza* was a cargo vessel that had been appraised of a tax by tax collector Whipple on a load of new cable it was carrying. The *Eliza*'s captain, Ladd, swore the cable was used goods and refused to pay. The ship and all of its cargo were impounded by the tax collector. It should have been an easy enough matter to sort out if the cable was new, old, taxable or not. But with Judge Pickering in charge of hearing the case, nothing was simple.

When Judge Pickering walked in for the day's first hearing on the case, he sat down, only to immediately adjourn, telling the assembled lawyers, witnesses and onlookers, "I'll be sober tomorrow; I am now damned drunk." Aside from the long-standing issues with Judge Pickering, some politics were about to come into play.

People today like to decry the divisive nature of politics and place blame squarely on the opposite political party, but this is no new phenomenon. People in Judge Pickering's time were no different. Partisan politics would have its fingers muddying the waters of *United States vs. The Eliza* from the very start. The district attorney and tax collector Whipple were both Republicans. The *Eliza*'s captain, Ladd, was the son of an influential political family of the Federalist persuasion. And Judge Pickering, like the captain of the *Eliza*, was a Federalist. On the second day of the trial, Judge Pickering showed up—maybe sober, maybe not—ready to give an immediate ruling on the case that he had not yet even heard one word about from either side. Without hearing from a single witness, reviewing a single document or letting the lawyers start their arguments, Judge Pickering favored fellow Federalist Captain Ladd, declaring the ship and all its cargo be returned immediately.

Of course, many cried foul. This kind of partisan politics was as unpopular then as it would be today. President Thomas Jefferson used the case as his basis to impeach Judge Pickering. There was a yearlong trial to remove the judge. His fear of crossing water continued even to this time, and Judge Pickering declined to attend his own trial to avoid traveling. In his place he sent one of his sons. But during the trial, even this son, acting in his father's stead, agreed under oath that Judge Pickering was insane. In a nineteen-to-seven vote, Judge Pickering was impeached, though it is worth noting that the vote fell along party lines. While Pickering was never convicted of a crime, his mental illness was enough to get him removed from the bench.

If the judge felt any shame, he did not have to grapple with it for very long. John Pickering died in Portsmouth on April 11, 1805, just short of a year after his impeachment.

5

ISLES OF SHOALS

The Isles of Shoals, in and of themselves, are pretty unexciting. They consist of a series of small islands, many that are more like small outcroppings of rock rather than proper islands, located just six to ten miles off the coast directly east of Portsmouth, New Hampshire. Half of the islands are considered to be part of New Hampshire, while the other half belong to Maine—though as you'll see even that gets complicated from time to time. From such an unassuming landscape, a wild wealth of history and legends has grown, some from before European settlers formed the state of New Hampshire.

Some sources say that the Native American tribes that called the mainland home refused to have anything to do with the Isles of Shoals, either because the islands were too sacred or too cursed to be trifled with. These stories seem to be a modern invention. The Natives both loved and feared the Isles of Shoals. Fishing was plentiful, but darker stories were told. The unforgiving landscape of the islands almost invites legends to be made up about them. This is in stark contrast to the glowing reviews given by Captain Smith, the first recorded European explorer to come across the islands. In fine Old-World tradition, he named them Smyth's Isles, after himself, and of them, he later wrote, "And of all the four parts of the world that I have yet seen not inhabited…I would rather live here than anywhere: and if it did not maintain itself, were we but once indifferently well fitted, let us starve."

But the discrepancy between the explorer's writing about the shoals and their more meager reality could be because Captain Smith just passed by the small group of islands and did not stop long enough to land on them. So, he was not as closely familiar with their peculiarities as those who came before and after him. Smith was mapping the Gulf of Maine at this time and had a bit of a romantic tinge to many of the things he wrote about the places he discovered.

When King James split up parts of New England, Captain Smith got his wish and was granted the islands he had named after himself. The final irony is that he'd never see the Isles of Shoals again and would die without ever having set foot on them. He tried four times to make the long journey from England to the Isles, and four times, he was turned back. Weather and pirates made the passage too dangerous. Captain Smith died in England in 1631, and the "Smythe Island" moniker faded from usage very quickly.

The first European explorers reached the islands and actually made landfall in 1623, when Captain Levett arrived with nearly three hundred men aboard six ships. To a man they marveled at just how inhospitable the Isles of Shoals were. Few trees could cling to the shallow ground that barely covered the rock. Storms would rage up suddenly and mercilessly. Of the shoals, Levett later wrote, "Upon these islands I neither could see one good timber-tree nor so much good ground as to make a garden. The place is found to be a good fishing-place for six ships, but more cannot be well there."

In 1628, the Isles of Shoals were used as a prison of sorts for just one man. Thomas Morton was exiled to them for his scandalous behavior in Massachusetts. Morton, a bawdy libertine, had a bit of a fascination with the Native cultures of the New World and a more than healthy interest in good old-fashioned partying. Morton and his friend Captain Wollaston created a trading post that scandalized their Puritan neighbors by trading both alcohol and guns to the Native population. While technically illegal, the practice was so widespread that it was only notable when Morton did it because of his reputation for trying to antagonize the local Puritan population. Then, as today, guns and beer were big business. Rather quickly, the trading post created by the two men became an outpost and then an agrarian colony whose ruling was based more on Morton's ideals than the usual styles of governorship of the time.

Despite having money pouring in, all was not well between Morton and Wollaston. Wollaston was selling off indentured servants as slaves to southern plantations, a practice that Morton was firmly against. Unable to convince his friend to stop, Morton planned an uprising. He convinced the

Right: This monument to Captain Smith was added to Star Island in 1846. Seacoast, New Hampshire, has called it "the ugliest monument in New Hampshire." *Photo by Renee Mallett.*

Below: Captain Levett did not look as favorably on the rocky shorelines of the Isles of Shoals as Captain Smith did before him. *Photo by Renee Mallett.*

remaining servants to pick up arms and drive Wollaston and the men loyal to him from the village. At that point, Morton took up leadership of the town. He renamed it Merrymount and declared that all remaining citizens were free men. The Native Americans were not forgotten by Morton when he took over leadership. He did his best to teach them his libertine ideals and continued to give them guns in exchange for food and furs.

The Puritans of the nearby Plimoth Bay Colony were not pleased. They told tales of orgies and accused Morton of going native. It's hard to say which accusation scandalized them more. The fact that Merrymount only continued to grow in wealth and size certainly didn't help the bad feelings of the Plymouth Colony. Morton, as you can probably guess, pressed the issue. In 1628, he threw a May Day party to end all parties, complete with odes to Greek gods and an eighty-foot-tall maypole that he topped with deer antlers. Myles Standish rallied the Plymouth Bay Colony Militia and took over Merrymount to save them from themselves. Morton was convicted of supplying firearms to the Natives. Because he was so well connected, the Plymouth Bay colonists feared executing him outright. Instead, they exiled him to the Isles of Shoals until such time that an English ship might arrive and save him from certain death.

In truth, the exile was meant to be a death sentence. Morton should have starved there or died from exposure. But stories of his kindness to the Native Americans had spread far and wide. The local Penacook tribe kept Morton alive until he rallied himself enough to return to the mainland. Morton went straight back to Merrymount but found the settlement renamed and his followers scattered. The party, it seemed, had ended for good. The Puritans wasted no time in arresting him again and banishing him from New England altogether.

Various small villages and communities have sprung up on the larger of the Isles of Shoals over the years. Appledore, claimed by Maine, is the largest of the island chain and the first to have a truly recognized town of any sort. Star Island, just 0.9 miles from Appledore but claimed by New Hampshire, would be home to the town of Gosport. But just who would decide to live on such tiny islands so close to the mainland but otherwise remote in every way? Characters, for the most part. Individuals who, even back then, felt the "Live Free or Die" motto deep in their bones, even if the words hadn't yet been uttered. Tax dodgers did so as well. Gosport was created when Massachusetts, which had claim of the area of Maine until the 1830s, tried to tax the Shoalers on Appledore. The residents, some forty or so families, simply packed up their belongings, rowed across the harbor and created the village on Star so they could continue on as they had been, now residents of tax-free New Hampshire.

Pirates also saw the appeal of the Isles of Shoals. Yes, like real pirates. Among many others during the golden age of piracy, Blackbeard, Captain Kidd and John Quelch, who would be hanged in Boston for his crimes at sea, all made stops at the Isles of Shoals. There have long been rumors of hidden pirate treasure on the islands that date from this time. In the summer of 1950, a group of adventurers traveled to Star Island with a device they said could be used to locate some of this long-rumored pirate gold. The group examined an aerial photograph of the forty-six-acre island and said definitively that $1 million worth of gold, rubies and diamonds, along with a mysterious eleven-foot-tall object, were located twenty-two feet below the topsoil. Despite these very specific measurements, the treasure hunters ultimately walked away empty-handed.

There is a breakwater connecting Star Island, Malaga Island and Smuttynose. It was constructed in several different parts over the past two hundred years but was started by Captain Samuel Haley to protect Gosport Harbor, which all of the islands surround. It is believed that Haley got the funds to build this breakwater when he discovered four bars of pirate's silver in his backyard in the Isles of Shoals.

It's said that pirates left not only treasure on the Isles of Shoals. Blackbeard is said to have divorced his fourteenth wife in a rather novel way. He left her on the shores of Lunging Island with an admonishment to watch over his treasure until he returned. But the young bride was left to watch for him all the rest of her days. Local legend says her ghost is still tied to this spot to watch for the adulterous sea captain.

The Revolutionary War caused an evacuation of the islands, though some of the staunch individualists who made up the shoals population refused to go. New Hampshire had some concerns about the political leanings of the Shoalers and used the excuse that they would be unable to protect the islands in the midst of a war to scatter the headstrong population among the mainland population. Things probably would have continued in this fashion, with the islands as a refuge for just a small number of eccentrics and fading into obscurity. It was a lighthouse that turned the islands into something more.

When Thomas Laighton accepted the two-year position of lighthouse keeper on White Island in 1839, he never could have guessed the way it would change the course of both his life and the future of the Isles of Shoals. Laighton didn't just see a job; he saw an opportunity. He bought Appledore

Thomas Laighton was paid an annual salary of $600 in 1839 to man the lighthouse on White Island. *Photo by Renee Mallett.*

Island and, in 1847, built a grand hotel there. In Laighton's case, it was truly a moment of "if you build it, they will come."

The real draw, however, wasn't the hotel and it wasn't the rich history of the island or its natural beauty. No, people flocked to Laighton's hotel because of his daughter, Celia Thaxter. Celia was just a child when her father moved her from Portsmouth to the Isles of Shoals. Many young women would have hated the isolation, but Celia loved it. At the age of sixteen, she married her father's business partner, Levi Thaxter, in the Appledore Hotel. The couple moved to the mainland, and it was Celia's first time there, apart from one year at a south Boston boarding school. She had three sons in rapid succession.

Celia wasn't content to be a typical 1800s housewife. In 1861, the *Atlantic Monthly* published her first poem, for which they paid her the lofty sum of ten dollars. Soon Celia Thaxter became an enormous literary presence, with many of her published works focused on her recollections of growing up on the Isles of Shoals.

If Celia's professional life was taking off, her private one was a series of struggles. Her marriage to Levi Thaxter was not a happy one. Their oldest son, Karl, suffered from a mental illness since early childhood and required a great deal of care. Celia separated from Levi and returned to Appledore Island with Karl in tow.

But the literary world did not forget Celia. With her as hostess of Appledore Island, it became an artists' colony of sorts, filled with all the notable artists and writers of her time. Nathaniel Hawthorne was a frequent visitor to Appledore, along with Ralph Waldo Emerson and Henry Wadsworth Longfellow. Impressionist painter Childe Hassam would not just visit, but some of his most famous works also feature Celia Laighton Thaxter among the flowers of her garden.

William Morris Hunt, the famed painter, made several trips to the Appledore Hotel. Sadly, not all of them were happy. In 1879, Celia discovered his body washed up on the shores of Appledore Island. It was a suicide. Hunt had spent several months on Appledore trying to overcome a serious depression and failed.

Celia Thaxter also died on Appledore Island, perhaps fittingly, as the Isles of Shoals were such a subject for her writing in life. On August 25, 1894, her body was discovered in the small cottage she lived in while running the hotel. She was buried nearby. Both her cottage and the Appledore Hotel burned to the ground in 1914.

Celia Laighton Thaxter's body is not the only one to be buried on the Isles of Shoals. For such tiny islands, there's a number of small cemeteries. On Star Island, right next to the Oceanic Hotel, which was built in 1873 to compete with Appledore Hotel, there's a small burying ground filled with members of the Caswell family. In the days when Shoalers first created Gosport, the Caswells were a prominent family. It's because of the Caswells that today's Oceanic Hotel survives at all. The original hotel was built by John Poore, but it burned in 1875, just a few short years after it was built. Undeterred, Poore combined several of the remaining Caswell family buildings into the current Oceanic Hotel. During more modern work on the Oceanic, a metal bar was found running underneath part of the structure—surviving evidence of how Caswell's Gosport house was lifted and moved next to Atlantic House.

In the middle of Star Island, buried under heaps of brush and wild growth, is the less well-known Beebe Cemetery. It has been called the most isolated cemetery in New Hampshire and was actually lost to history for many years. It's easy, considering it consists of just three small graves belonging to a group of young sisters who lost their lives to diphtheria all within a few days of one another.

If anything, it's surprising there aren't more burying grounds on the Isles of Shoals. Deaths, particularly violent ones, have been fixtures in the history

Celia Thaxter's cottage on Appledore Island was lost to the same fire that took her father's hotel. *Library of Congress public domain.*

The Oceanic Hotel was built on the remains of the original hotel, which burned shortly after being built. The use of fire is severely restricted to this day in and around the hotel. *Photo by Renee Mallett.*

of this place. Today, when tourists come to Star Island, they usually make a stop at Betty Moody's Cave. The cave itself isn't much to look at—like a little cubby hole in the rocky shore. It's the story of Betty Moody that draws them here. In 1724, the Isles of Shoals came under attack during Lovewell's War. Betty Moody grabbed her three small children and hid in the cave that would later be named after her. She survived the attack from the Native Americans but found, after they left, that she had smothered her smallest child to death while trying to quiet his cries.

A less well-known Star Island landmark is Miss Underhill's Chair. Nancy Underhill was a teacher in Gosport in the 1850s. What became known as her chair was an outcropping of rock, where, nightly, she would take a walk and stop to read from her Bible. But one evening she was snatched from the rocks by the sea and swept away. Shoalers searched for the unfortunate Miss Underhill, but there was no trace of her until nearly a week later when her body washed up in York, Maine. The Underhill family claimed the body and transported it to Chester, New Hampshire, for a proper burial.

The Underhill family had another unique connection to death on the Isles of Shoals. The same year that John Poore was trying to outshine Appledore Hotel with the creation of the Oceanic and Celia Thaxter was bringing notables from around the country to visit the islands, national media attention was focused on the Isles of Shoals for a much darker reason.

The sad tale began in 1868, when a Norwegian couple immigrated to Smuttynose Island. At the time, John Hontvet and his wife, Maren, were the only full-time residents on the island. The entire population of all the Isles of Shoals only numbered around fifty at this time. The Hontvets came, like so many before them, for the plentiful fish that could be caught around the Isles of Shoals. John Hontvet was an industrious fisherman who spent every day at sea catching everything he could before heading to Portsmouth to sell the day's catch and buy his bait for the next day.

By May 1871, the Hontvets had prospered enough that they sent for Maren's sister. Karen Christensen, recently widowed, was happy to come live with her sister in their little red cottage on the shores of Smuttynose. She quickly gained employment as a maid on Appledore and settled into the life of a Shoaler. Karen wasn't the only addition to the Isles of Shoals. A German-born fisherman named Louis Wagner arrived around the same time.

If Karen Christensen was welcomed by the Shoalers, Louis Wagner most definitely was not. People found him unusual. They felt that he hovered around the corners of rooms, always watching and listening but never joining in. Where he came from or why he moved was never shared with

Smuttynose Island, as seen from Star Island, was the scene of a grisly murder in 1873 that would go on to inspire Anita Shreve's book *The Weight of Water*. *Photo by Renee Mallett.*

his new neighbors. This was one aspect about Wagner that didn't raise the alarm bells the way it might have on the mainland. Over the years, after all, many people had come to the Isles of Shoals to leave their pasts behind.

The Hontvets did not share the Shoalers' misgivings about Wagner. The couple took him in, giving him a bed to sleep in, clothing to wear and a hot meal every night. Though he was a muscular twenty-eight-year-old, Wagner couldn't make ends meet on his own as a fisherman. John Hontvet was doing so well that he hired Wagner. But in October 1872, John Hontvet suddenly found himself with more help than he needed. Both his brother and Maren's brother came from Norway to live with them on Smuttynose. Maren's brother, Ivan, even arrived with a newlywed wife, Anethe.

It was a lot of people in one small island cottage and a lot of big men to manage one fishing boat. After five weeks of this arrangement, the Hontvets decided Louis Wagner would have to go. They didn't want to leave their friend with no way to make his way in the world though. So, the Hontvets helped Wagner secure employment on a passing fishing boat named the *Addison Gilbert*, thanked him for his help and congratulated themselves that they had helped their friend get back on his feet.

If the Hontvets were pleased with the arrangement, Wagner was less so. Shortly after taking up a position on the crew of the *Addison Gilbert*, the ship was wrecked. Wagner found himself in Portsmouth in even more dire straits than he had been during his early times on Smuttynose. Wagner found what work he could on the wharves, but his strange demeanor made it unlikely that even a desperate sea captain would hire him for any kind of a long journey. It was a catch-as-catch-can life, and Wagner found himself resenting the Hontvets more and more for sending him away from their comfortable cottage.

On March 5, 1873, John Hontvet saw Wagner for the first time since watching his large figure fade from view on the deck of the *Addison Gilbert*. Hontvet, joined by his brother and brother-in-law, were tying up at the dock in Portsmouth when they ran into Louis Wagner. Wagner asked the men if they were staying overnight in the city, and they told him they were. The shipment of bait they needed for fishing the next day was late, and it made more sense at this point to collect the shipment, prepare their trawl lines and return home the next evening. Hontvet, seeing how ragged his old friend looked, offered him an evening's work. Wagner said he would bait the trawl lines while the men found rooms for themselves in town.

But Wagner had no intention of spending his evening tying stinking bait to the lines. Knowing that all of the men from the Smuttynose cottage would be on the mainland for the night, he concocted a scheme to get to the island and rob the Hontvet home. Wagner stole a flat-bottomed rowboat and headed out into the dark, moonless night.

Twelve miles of rowing would have been too much for most men, but Wagner had arms conditioned from years of work on fishing boats and docks. He made short work of the estimated three-hour trip. He approached the cottage from the backside of the island, watching carefully as the women inside turned out the lights and went to bed. He gave them some time and approached the house as silently as possible.

He found the door unlocked, as one would expect at that time on a nearly uninhabited island. Wagner snuck inside and wedged a piece of wood into the door, blocking Maren Hontvet's bedroom from the common spaces of the cottage. She and her sister-in-law, Anethe, were effectively locked inside. Just then the small dog that Maren had kept as a pet for many years began to bark.

All three women, Maren and Anethe in the bedroom and Karen asleep on the couch, woke. Wagner panicked, grabbed a nearby chair and started to beat Karen into silence, even while the women locked inside the adjoining room began to scream. In a final grasp to live, Karen threw herself at the bedroom door and pulled the piece of wood from the latch. Wagner tried to follow her inside, but the three terrified women were able to bolt the door from the inside before he did.

Anethe made for the room's only window. She was standing barefoot in the remains of the March snow when Louis Wagner came around the corner of the house. She had just enough time to recognize him before he grabbed the Underhill Edge Tool Company axe, made by relatives of Gosport schoolteacher Nancy Underhill, from the nearby woodpile. He raised the axe and split her head with one blow.

Maren, seeing Anethe was dead, checked on her sister. Karen, she realized, was beyond saving. The axe had just started its work against her locked bedroom door when Maren followed Anethe's doomed path out the window and into the cold night air. Realizing that Wagner would be as familiar with the few small buildings on Smuttynose as she was, Maren headed toward the cove, hoping to take the killer's boat for her own and flee to the safety of the surrounding islands. She didn't account for Wagner approaching from sea by the far side of the island the way he had. Seeing no way to leave the confines of Smuttynose, she wedged herself between two rocks and hoped the moonless night and the sound of the sea would be enough to hide her from Wagner.

It was Maren's one stroke of luck. Wagner searched for her in every place he could think of but never imagined she'd be half drenched in saltwater beneath some stones at the water's edge. He ransacked the Hontvet home, finding only fifteen dollars for his trouble, and made himself something to eat.

The sun was up for hours before Maren could convince herself to come out from her hiding place. Barefoot, she staggered across the breakwater and called for help. A fellow Norwegian immigrant saw her distress and brought her to his house on Appledore before gathering a group of armed men to search Smuttynose. There was no sign of Wagner. The bodies of the two women were discovered just as their husbands and John Hontvet returned home.

Wagner fled for Boston after rowing back to the mainland. But he wasn't free for long. John Hontvet was able to give a very good description of the murderer to the police, considering the man had been his neighbor or lived with him for several years. When the Boston police transported Wagner back to Portsmouth for trial, a mob of ten thousand people was waiting for him, screaming insults and swearing they would execute him themselves if they could.

Wagner swore his innocence, but after nine days of trial and not even an hour of deliberation, a jury found him guilty of both murders. He escaped jail just a week after sentencing, but by that point, he was one of the most infamous figures in the state. Wagner couldn't hide for long before authorities had him back in confinement again. On June 25, 1875, he was hanged from the gallows in a prison in Thomaston, Maine. He would be the last person to be executed in the state of Maine.

The remaining Hontvets couldn't bear to return to the Isles of Shoals. John remained a prosperous fisherman, but he did it from a home in Portsmouth, not the Smuttynose cottage. Anathe's husband found work as a carpenter on Appledore, but after just one year, he found his love for the shoals had turned. He returned to Norway and was never seen again.

The story of the Smuttynose murders is one that has long-reaching appeal, even to audiences today. Anita Shreve's book *The Weight of Water* is based on the crime, though she makes the case that Wagner was wrongly convicted. The book spawned a film adaptation in 2000, though it was filmed in Nova Scotia, not the Isles of Shoals. Shreve was not the first writer intrigued by the events of 1873. The crimes are featured in the John Perrault song "The Ballad of Louis Wagner." No less an authority on the shoals than Celia Thaxter would also write about the crime in her story "A Memorable Murder."

Today you won't find any killers on the Isles of Shoals. In modern times, they might be as uninhabited as at any other time in their history. Lunging Island is privately owned. White Island features one of only two lighthouses on the New Hampshire coast, but it's fully automated now. Appledore Island is owned by the Star Island Corporation. Although it is the largest of the Isles of Shoals, most of the buildings on it have been lost over the years to weather and fire. It is the home of the Isles of Shoals Marine Laboratory, which operates in a collaboration between the University of New Hampshire and Cornell University. The Star Island Corporation, as you can probably guess, also owns Star Island. The Oceanic Hotel is still in operation; it's the center of a series of summer retreats run every year by the Unitarian Universalist Church. It is kept, in as many ways as possible, just as it was during its heyday. While guests come for weeklong retreats in painting, art, yoga and other exploration, they eat family-style meals in the sprawling dining room, have candle-lit services in the 150-year-old stone church and duck seagulls and poison ivy, just as the Shoalers of years past

Tucks Monument is often mistaken as a monument to Captain Smith. It honors 1700s preacher Reverend John Tuck. *Photo by Renee Mallett.*

Stone cottages on Star Island. Photo by Renee Mallett.

Left: The original chapel on Star Island was burned as firewood in 1790 by Shoalers. The current chapel is made of stone and is more than 150 years old. *Photo by Renee Mallett.*

Below: The turnstile harkens back to a time when Star Island was used as grazing land. *Photo by Renee Mallett.*

did before them. Day-trippers are welcome to the island as long as the boats from the Isles of Shoals Steamship Company are running. In the winter, a single caretaker lives on Star Island, keeping watch over the hotel and the grounds where pirates, murderers and tax dodgers once lived.

6

LOVEWELL'S WAR

*W*hile men like Thomas Morton may have tried to befriend the Native populations during the early years of the creation of New England, not many took that path. Relations between the Native tribes and the European settlers were often blood-soaked and questionable in New Hampshire's earliest days.

In 1691, thirty to forty Abenaki warriors approached New Hampshire by canoe. They came across a group of settlers cutting hay in the salt marshes along the shore. What followed would be a heart-breaking massacre. Twenty-one settlers, mostly women and children, were taken prisoner by the Abenaki or killed outright. The few small cabins were burned to the ground, and the remains of the villagers were left, bloodied, where they had fallen.

When the attack was discovered, the victims of the Brackett Massacre were buried in the spot where they had died. Today the area, tiny in size, is tucked away in the woods at the side of a residential road with just a single wooden sign to mark the spot.

It was growing up with stories like these that informed young John Lovewell's opinions of the Native populations. This Nashua, New Hampshire–born militia figure went on to become a hero of his day for the fights he led against the Abenaki tribe. But history has a way of turning on even the most beloved figures. In modern times, the view of Lovewell is far more controversial.

John Lovewell didn't just defend himself against attacks, but he also aggressively went after the Natives. And one of the things he was most

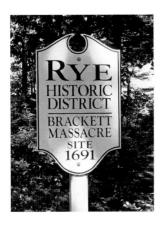

The twenty or so people killed in the Brackett Massacre are buried where they were killed, just between this sign and the nearby salt marsh. *Photo by Renee Mallett.*

celebrated for in his day—taking numerous scalps—is not seen as the mark of a hero in modern times. Born in 1691 in present-day Nashua, Lovewell was, and would continue to be, the most famous scalp hunter of his time.

But all of the scalps and the many forays he ran against the Abenaki as a militia captain would also be his undoing. Lovewell was in Maine hunting down more Natives with a band of thirty-six men when the party stopped to exchange fire with a lone Abenaki warrior. While Lovewell traded shots, an entire war party of Abenaki arrived. Eight of the militia men, including John Lovewell himself, were killed in the first volley of shots.

Ultimately, the battle raged for eleven hours. Only twenty of the militia survived by the time an errant bullet killed the great War Chief Paugus, causing the rest of the tribe to scatter. On the retreat home to New Hampshire, three more of the militia party would join John Lovewell in the grave.

Lovewell's widow and children were given prime farmland in what is now Pembroke, New Hampshire, as a thank-you for his service. Lovewell Mountain in Washington, New Hampshire, would be named after the famed ranger, as well as several natural landmarks in Maine. Nathaniel Hawthorne, Henry Wadsworth Longfellow and Henry David Thoreau all knew of Lovewell and his single-minded war against the Abenaki. All three famous writers would pen stories inspired by the tale.

7

AMERICA'S STONEHENGE

merica's Stonehenge might seem like an unusual addition to a book full of scandalous history. The spot is one of the most popular tourist attractions in the state of New Hampshire and has even been featured on the American History Channel's show *Secrets of the Ancient World*. The site is most famous, of course, for its odd stone groupings, but the fun family attraction also features hiking trails, snow shoeing and some absolutely adorable alpacas. However, the history behind the off-beat tourist hot spot involves a fair amount of good old-fashioned greed—enough that to this day the true purpose of the stone monoliths is obscured and disputed.

If you come expecting thirteen-foot-high standing stones like the more famous prehistoric site in England, you'll be disappointed. But the stone groupings at the Salem, New Hampshire attraction still have a charm all their own. They create peculiar little cubbies, tight walkways and a labyrinthine maze of rock to be traversed, climbed and puzzled over.

The first obvious mention of the odd stone structures scattered across some thirty acres of land can be traced to the 1907 book *History of Salem, New Hampshire* by Edgar Gilbert. He referred to the stones as "Johnathon Pattee's Cave." John Pattee farmed the land seventy years before the publication of Mr. Gilbert's book. He was a well-respected farmer of middling income who was best known not for owning an Americanized version of Stonehenge but for taking in the destitute. Today there are those who believe that Farmer Pattee built the structures himself, using them for storage and root cellars during his ownership of the farm.

The Stonehenge in England is one of the world's most famous prehistoric monuments, but it is not the only ancient collection of stones. *Photo by Renee Mallett.*

Others have attributed much different origins to the stones. There are those who feel the site was created long before the arrival of Christopher Columbus, though no artifacts exist on-site to back up these ideas. Others feel they have a purpose similar to that of the much more famous Stonehenge in England and that they were used as some sort of astrological calendar by an as yet unidentified Bronze Age people. In modern times, the New Age and Neo-Pagan communities have supported this idea and have been granted use of the site for key celebrations throughout the year.

The reason for all of the confusion can be traced pretty directly to one man, William Goodwin. Goodwin purchased the property in 1937 and christened it with the spooky-sounding name "Mystery Hill." Goodwin charged visitors to tour the property. He worked tirelessly to popularize the idea that the stone markers were linked to Irish Culdee Monks who he said built a monastery and worked the property long before Columbus ever came to America. It's unclear whether Goodwin believed this or if it was simply a good story that he came up with to pull in tourists. In an effort to back up this claim, Goodwin moved many of the stones from their original positions, built new caves and gave many of them fanciful names such as "Sacrificial Stone."

Goodwin, an insurance executive with no formal archaeology training, spent roughly twenty years digging out more caves and moving stones into what he said were the original locations of the Culdee monastery. If the blame for much of the confusion can be laid at Goodwin's feet, there have certainly been other amateur historians who have had their hands in interpreting the site. Mystery Hill would contribute to the downfall of Barry Fell. Fell was a well-respected authority on marine invertebrates who would go on to face the utter rejection of the scientific community when he began publishing books on his pseudo archaeological theory that Celts, Basques, Phoenicians and ancient Egyptians were extensively colonizing America long before Columbus. Fell claimed to have found epigraphs at Mystery Hill that he was sure came from Iberian Celts. The problem is that Fell was a marine biologist, not a trained historian or archaeologist, and no authorities on the subjects of Iberian Celts, Phoenicians or the like support his assertions that the marks he found have anything at all to do with those cultures. Undeterred, Fell included his claims about America's Stonehenge in his book *America B.C.* Though the book was popular enough, it was skewered by the scientific community and book reviewers alike. One 1977 *New York Times* article by Cambridge University archaeology professor Glyn Daniel about the rise of what he called "rubbish off-archaeology books" criticized Fell and his claims about Mystery Hill. Daniel, an authority on the topic of archaeology, lumped Fell in with other "non establishment, tragic-comic, and misinformed writers."

In 1957, Goodwin leased the land to Robert Stone. Stone bought the land outright ten years later, and his family continues to operate the attraction to this day. The Stones have been better stewards of the site than Goodwin. They changed the name from Mystery Hill to America's Stonehenge, adding a museum and gift shop, plus the alpacas, but overall leaving the stones and existing caves where they found them. They have been respectful of the pagan communities' wishes to celebrate the site, even while encouraging true archaeological exploration.

In his book *The Archaeology of New Hampshire: Exploring 10,000 Years in the Granite State*, archaeologist David Starbuck says Goodwin "created much of what is visible at the site today." Starbuck elaborated, "The moment the first stone was moved to a new location by William Goodwin, the entire site lost any chance of being taken seriously by scholarly community."

That's not to say that no true archaeologists have ever had a hand in trying to untangle the mystery at Mystery Hill. There have been legitimate archaeological excavations over the years at America's Stonehenge that have turned up plenty of evidence of eighteenth- and nineteenth-century habitation by Native Americans and farmers such as Johnathon Pattee. More compelling to many of the site's visitors is the feeling the place gives them. It is undeniable that it is a peaceful oasis with some lovely views of New Hampshire's natural beauty, dotted here and there with stone monoliths and a network of caves, crevices and nooks that have inspired speculation and wonder for at least the past one hundred years.

8

MYSTERY STONE

*I*n a place known as the Granite State, there shouldn't be anything particularly interesting about a stone. But, as seen in the last chapter, New Hampshire has some strange history with some odd stones—and oftentimes there's someone in the background trying to find a way to capitalize on the mystery. When it comes to the rock pulled from the ground by Seneca Augustus Ladd in Meredith in the 1870s, the one thing for sure is that it wasn't the typical old hunk of New Hampshire granite.

A group of laborers hired by Seneca Ladd pulled the stone from six feet below the Earth's surface while digging postholes for a fence in Meredith, New Hampshire. To be sure, they probably pulled a lot of rocks from the ground while putting in Seneca Ladd's fence. But none of the others were like this. Four inches high and two and a half inches wide at its deepest point, the egg-shaped stone would have been something to talk about even if it hadn't been covered in strange carvings. The oblong stone, weighing just over a pound, is perfectly smooth and is a uniformly dark color. One side features the calming visage of a human face. Around the rest are squiggles, dots, corn, arrows, a moon and other more abstract human figures. The stone is bored through from bottom to top, like a very heavy oversized bead, though one end of the smooth channel is larger than the other, as if bored by different-sized bits. It would be easy to pass this off as modern-day defacement of a much older relic, but some of the carvings surrounding the holes give the impression that it was done when the egg was first created. Modern analysis shows the stone was carved from quartzite, which is not normally found in the ground in New Hampshire.

Speculation about the true purpose of the stone has always been a popular pastime. The more credible theories say it was made at some unknown historical date to commemorate a peace treaty between two Native American tribes. The hole could have been drilled for the egg to be placed on a stake marking a territorial boundary between two places. Some foreign stone egg researchers believe there is a Celtic or Inuit origin. Other stranger and more otherworldly origins have been suggested. While the stone may be a singular find in New Hampshire, similar stone eggs, with similar odd little carvings, have been found from time to time across the globe. New Hampshire's stone was the first found in the United States.

Of course, true lovers of odd and unusual history have probably already noted that the discovery of this strange little artifact came just a few years after that of the Cardiff Giant. The Cardiff Giant was a seemingly petrified ten-foot-tall man who was discovered by some laborers digging a well for one Mr. William C. Newell in Cardiff, New York. The mummy attracted gawkers by the wagonload, who paid twenty-five to fifty cents each to get a look at it. Mr. Newell, as you can imagine, made a mint. The interest didn't die down, even when the giant was revealed to be a hoax perpetrated by Mr. Newell's cousin George Hull. Hull had spent $2,600 creating the desiccated figure out of a block of gypsum that was quarried from Iowa, shipped to New York by train and given an ancient-looking color with the use of acids and stains before being buried in his cousin's backyard. In today's dollars, this would be the equivalent of nearly $48,000. Hull, a militant atheist, had dreamed up the scheme after arguing with a preacher over the mention of giants in the Bible. Hull, it seems, would go to great lengths to embarrass others.

In the end, it was actually a pretty good investment for Hull and his cousin Newell. Besides the coins paid by the curious, they sold the giant for close to $50,000 ($456,000 by today's standards). P.T. Barnum tried to purchase the giant to add to his collection of sideshow wonders, but the board that had bought the Cardiff Giant from Hull refused to sell it. Barnum wasn't deterred. He went to great lengths to covertly make a mold of the giant and showcased his wax replica to great fanfare. The matter went to court, and the battle got pretty heated before George Hull decided to fess up to his ruse. It's been called the most famous hoax in American history and is so popular even today that no fewer than three Cardiff Giants can be found on display at various museums. The Farmer's Museum in Cooperstown, New York, has the original Cardiff Giant, while a museum of oddities known as Marvin's Marvelous Mechanical Museum displays what they say is Barnum's replica, and the Fort Museum and

Frontier Village in Iowa shows off a replica of the replica. Sometimes a swindle can be big business, even after its deception comes to light.

With the nationwide attention the Cardiff Giant garnered when it was discovered, and the high price tag that came when it was sold, it's not too far of a reach for some that maybe the Mystery Egg was another hoax dreamed up in the hopes of cashing in. It would seem that if the stone was a hoax, then Seneca Ladd might have been the target and not the perpetrator. Ladd dubbed the egg the "Mystery Stone of Lake Winnipesaukee" and quite genuinely seemed to believe that it was some unknowable "Indian" relic. He kept the stone, which garnered a fair amount of attention when it was discovered, until his death, when it was passed along to his relative Francis Ladd Coe, who lived in Center Harbor. Francis, in turn, passed the strange little egg to one of his daughters, who eventually handed it off to the New Hampshire Historical Society. It remains on view in the museum to this day.

9

OLD MAN IN THE MOUNTAIN

On the subject of tourist attractions and rocks, you can't talk about New Hampshire without mentioning the Old Man in the Mountain. This forty-foot-tall stone face, composed of five granite cliffs and ledges, once graced the side of Cannon Mountain. That the ledges looked like a face depended on where you were standing, with the profile being most pronounced when viewed from the north.

The great stone face has been used as an emblem for the state since 1946, when it started being featured on the state's road signs and license plates. A viewing area was built for the face so that tourists could be sure to see it from its best side, and the Old Man even makes an appearance on the New Hampshire state quarter that came out in the year 2000.

When the stone face collapsed on May 3, 2003, it's fair to say that people in New Hampshire were pretty upset. A taskforce headed by a former governor even considered the idea of creating a replica face to erect in the spot where the old one had stood. Even after the idea was rejected by the taskforce, nonprofit groups were formed to continue to look into the idea. Money was raised to install coin-operated viewfinders at the base of Cannon Mountain, where curious tourists can spend a few quarters to see how the face once looked. Since 2003, several different schemes have been proposed, and ultimately rejected, concerning restoring, replacing and otherwise replicating the Old Man in the Mountain.

Detractors of these plans have always said it's foolish to try to create an inauthentic attraction from what nature first made. But the thing they, and most visitors to the Old Man in the Mountain when he still stood, don't seem to know is that the face was never truly a purely natural occurrence. The face was first described by a surveying team in Franconia Notch in 1805. Daniel Webster, the great American statesman, popularized the face. It even acted as muse to Nathaniel Hawthorne when the author wrote his story "The Great Stone Face" in 1850.

Even in those early stages of the stone face's time as a tourist attraction, it had gotten a face-lift of sorts. Some early reports say it was dynamited to make the outline of the face more pronounced. By 1920, large chains were holding the stones into place to help visitors make out the visage. In 1957, the state legislature appropriated $25,000 toward facial reconstruction on a massive scale. This included the use of twenty tons of cement and steel rods, as well as the creation of a rain gutter. From that time on, a team of people from the State Highway and Park division took care of the face as part of a schedule of routine maintenance.

So, while Hawthorne may have waxed poetic about "a work of Nature in her mood of majestic playfulness," when talking about the Old Man in the Mountain and detractors of plans to reconstruct the face after the 2003 collapse because it wasn't authentic enough, they weren't taking into consideration the extensive man-made enhancements the attraction had already undergone over the years.

In June 2011, a memorial park was dedicated on the shore of Profile Lake, not far from where the viewing area once attracted curious visitors. As of 2019, most talk of rebuilding and reconstruction has long faded away.

10

ROCK RIMMON

nother thing often overlooked by fans of Franconia Notch's Old Man in the Mountain is that while it may be the best-known stone face in New Hampshire, it is certainly not the only one. Mount Liberty in Franconia Notch State Park was given its name because early settlers thought it looked like George Washington lying face-up. Franconia Notch State Park even features an Old Lady of the Mountain. This face on Mount Lafayette is sometimes called the Watcher because her face is bent down to look back at visitors. Not to be outdone, Jackson, New Hampshire's Iron Mountain has a duck's face on the eastern side.

And then there's Manchester's Rock Rimmon. Many stone ledges in New Hampshire have been given the name Rock Rimmon as homage to the biblically famous stone near Jerusalem. Manchester's Rock Rimmon may not have a unique name, but it certainly has one of the most interesting histories of all of New Hampshire's stones.

Manchester's Rock Rimmon is a roughly 300-foot-wide, 150-foot-long cliff that looms darkly over Rock Rimmon Park. That it is dark is not just the opinion of this author. A 1915 account of the rock in the now-defunct *Amoskeag Bulletin* describes it as being "like some proud tombstone of the mighty dead."

Part of the deathly connotation might have something to do with the rock's history as a lover's leap. An early legend about the cliff dating to the American Revolution tells the sad, though apocryphal, tale of a noble young Englishman who came to the New World to educate the Penacook

Rock Rimmon as seen from Rock Rimmon Park. Unusual stories have always been linked to this outcropping of rock. *Photo by Renee Mallett.*

Natives. While living among the Native people, this nobleman fell in love with Raymond, one of the maidens in the village. The girl, it is said, loved him just as much.

One evening, the Englishman asked Raymond to meet him atop Rock Rimmon. Watching the sunset, he convinced his love to follow him to England. But some of the tribesmen overheard this plan and became enraged. As the young maiden left to pack her things for the long journey across the ocean, her brothers attacked her lover and threw his body from the cliff. When Raymond discovered what they had done, she threw herself from the cliff so that in death they could be together the way they could not be in life.

Some versions of this myth take the story several steps further. They say that the tribe soon left the area near the rock, either because it was haunted by the star-crossed lovers or because hunting started to go badly for them here. The tribe gathered any tools or weapons they could part with and secured them inside a cave located in the rock so they could move quickly to a new village without being weighed down by too many things.

Geologically, this seems as unlikely as a Penacook maiden with the name of Raymond. Geologists have never found any evidence that there are or ever were caves in Rock Rimmon. But that hasn't stopped some treasure hunters or hobbyist archaeologists from trying their luck at finding this hidden cache, despite the dangers of looking. There's been many injuries and a few deaths on Rock Rimmon, ranging from an eight-year-old boy who had serious but not life-threatening leg injuries to an eighteen-year-old man who fell to his death while his two horror-struck friends watched. In 1992, the *Union Leader* reported that a young man who described himself as "not a novice climber" got stuck while traversing Rock Rimmon. Police were called to help him down. But it's unclear how many of these people were there looking for lost treasure and who could have been there for other purposes. For a while, the top of the rock was a popular, if risky, hangout spot for Manchester's teens.

But it's when you move away from the realms of myth and legend and into that of history that you find some truly strange tales of this seemingly average stone outcropping in a state that has more than its fair share of them. In many ways, it would probably be just as apt to call Rock Rimmon the "mystery stone" instead of the egg-shaped artifact in the New Hampshire Historical Society Museum. Death has always surrounded Rock Rimmon. An August 12, 1857 edition of the *Manchester American* shares the story of thirteen-year-old Geo F. Barry. He was picking blueberries at the base of Rock Rimmon when an oddly colored snake, said to be six feet in length, attacked him. His companion, a small, scrappy dog, saw his owner's distress and fought the snake off. Both the boy and his pet made it home, scared but unscathed. Ten days later, the teen boy died suddenly. Records show his death resulted from dysentery, a common enough occurrence for the time, but the boy had shown no symptoms until he died.

In 1876, an older teen, named George Morgan, got lock jaw and died after accidentally shooting himself on Rock Rimmon. He had no explanation for what he was doing there with the shotgun that day or how he had managed to harm himself with it.

But the eeriest story of all about Rock Rimmon is the story of the face. In 1911, the rock and the land surrounding it had been given by the Amoskeag Manufacturing Company to the City of Manchester to use as a park in perpetuity for the bargain basement price of one dollar. The move from private property to public park wasn't much of a stretch. Regardless of who owned the land, it had been a popular gathering and picnicking spot for many years. In 1925, state forestry commissioner John Corliss was reevaluating the park and "discovered" that Rock Rimmon had a stone face not unlike the famous one in Franconia Notch. The profile was so clear and distinct that it seemed impossible that no one had ever reported it before. Several newspapers reported the story, showing photographs of the Old Man of Rock Rimmon side by side with photos of the Old Man formation in Franconia Notch. Compared to the other, it was striking just how easy it was to see the face on Rock Rimmon.

Rock Rimmon Park was gifted to the City of Manchester for just one dollar and a promise that it would always be open to the public. *Photo by Renee Mallett.*

The Parks Commission began drawing up plans for viewing platforms, hoping that the Old Man in Rock Rimmon would do for Manchester's tourist trade what the Old Man in the Mountain had done for the north country. These plans were quickly scrapped when, inexplicably, no one could find the face anymore.

With no signs or reports of landslides or collapse, one day the face just couldn't be picked out of the rock anymore. Although photos of the formation survive, the exact spot where one would have to stand to see it no longer seems to be recorded anywhere. As much as people have tried poking around for lost Native American caches, even more have tried to find the face that didn't exist, existed and then was lost again.

11

CEMETERIES

CHESTER VILLAGE CEMETERY

One of the state's oldest and most famous burial grounds is found in the small town of Chester, New Hampshire. The Chester Village Cemetery is located at the intersection of Raymond Road and Chester Street, more or less smack-dab in the middle of the town. The small but sprawling cemetery has been in use since 1751 and features a number of notable inhabitants, including two governors, a chief justice of the New Hampshire Supreme Court and a famed 1800s clockmaker. But in the Chester Village Cemetery, some graves are more famous for what can be found on the stones than for who is buried beneath them.

Many famous stone carvers have their work on display in Chester Village Cemetery. Gravestone rubbers come from all over New England to capture images from the Revolutionary War–period stones that helped the cemetery secure itself a spot in the National Register of Historic Places in 1979. Some of the most sought-after gravestones are not collected for their age or even their pedigree but rather because they were carved by Stephen or Abel Webster.

These two brothers were both Chester residents and prominent stone carvers in their day. Early American tombstones created during their lifetimes had some common motifs. Weeping willow trees and smiling beatific angels graced many tombstones in this time period. Look at pretty much any of the stones carved by Abel, and you're sure to see some classic

Left: Grim-faced gravestones were not appreciated by the villagers of Chester, who felt they might be a reflection on what the stone carver felt about their dearly departed family. *Photo by Renee Mallett.*

Below: A more traditional gravestone. This one is in Point of Graves Cemetery in Portsmouth, New Hampshire. *Photo by Renee Mallett.*

Right: Weeping willow trees were a common tombstone motif for many years. *Photo by Renee Mallett.*

Below: One of the unhappy figures found in Chester Village Cemetery. *Photo by Renee Mallett.*

examples of chubby-cheeked little cherubs showing their joy at one more soul ascending to heaven.

Then there are the stones carved by his equally talented brother, Stephen. Some of the stones also feature the classic smiling angel. But more than a few feature a different sort of expression altogether. In fact, many of these figures are downright grim and frowning. This might not seem like a big deal today, but in the late 1700s and early 1800s, this caused quite the uproar.

Because no one was quite sure why Stephen carved smiles on some tombstones and frowns on others, one can't help but speculate that he was trying to say something about the person the stone was commemorating. Some stories say the stone carver had a religious conversion in the later years of his life, which spurred his ill will toward his neighbors. Another popular theory is that the faces say something about how quickly the bereaved family members of the deceased paid Webster's bill.

Among the graves in the Chester Village Cemetery, you can find those of the Webster brothers. Abel died in 1801, and his well-worn gravestone features an urn, another classic icon for tombstones in his day. Stephen outlived his brother by a number of years and also has a staid engraving on his marker, in this case a hand pointing upward in the direction that his spirit hopefully went.

OLD CEMETERY

Chester is not the only town in New Hampshire with notable, unique graves. The small town of Washington, New Hampshire, might be home to just over 1,100 people, but it has some unusual folks taking up residence at one of the cemeteries in town.

In 1804, a local tavern owner by the name of Captain Samuel Jones had the misfortune of getting his leg pinned between a fence and a building he was helping to move. Local stories say Captain Jones and his friends enjoyed the fruits of the tavern's storeroom while waiting for the doctor to arrive. When he arrived, despite the revelry, the doctor had grave news for Captain Jones. The leg could not be saved and was amputated on the spot.

Whether Captain Jones was still under the influence or because he gave credence to a bit of folk wisdom that said treating an amputated limb with reverence would lessen the phantom pains in the future, he decided to hold a full funeral for his leg. In fact, Captain Jones had it buried with full honors in Old Cemetery on Faxon Hill Road and erected a tombstone for it. The simple inscription reads, "Captain Samuel Jones leg which was amputated July 7, 1804."

By the time the captain passed many years later, he had moved from New Hampshire. Reports differ about whether he was a resident of Boston, Rhode Island or New York at the time of his death. One thing is for sure: only Captain Jones's leg is buried in New Hampshire. The rest of him is believed to be interred in the Bronx, New York, giving Captain Jones the unlikely honor of being one of probably only a few people buried in more than one state.

Local lore around the town of Washington says that at one point college students made off with the tombstone of Captain Jones's leg. Eventually, the police tracked it down, decorating a dorm room, and returned it to its proper plot in Old Cemetery.

The gravestone of Captain Jones's leg is not the only eyebrow-raising one in that graveyard. The stone that marks the final resting places of Fred and Elba Chase, who passed in 1933 and 1967, respectively, features an engraving of a Russian hammer and sickle. The stone further specifies that the Chases were "courageous and devoted fighters in the class struggle."

12

ALEISTER CROWLEY'S RETIREMENT

*A*leister Crowley came from a devout Christian family and was educated at the University of Cambridge. From there, it was probably expected that he would marry well and carry on with the typical life of a wealthy English son. Instead, he gained worldwide infamy as a bisexual drug user and Satanist. Or, as many newspapers would sum him up in life, "the wickedest man in the world." Crowley's interest in the arcane seems to have started in childhood but really took hold during his Cambridge years when he started practicing ritual magic with the secret society known as the Hermetic Order of the Golden Dawn. Other notable Golden Dawn members who Crowley rubbed shoulders with include *Dracula* author Bram Stoker, Irish revolutionary Maud Gonne and the famed poet W.B. Yeats.

Crowley was a social critic and many times over published writer. He was also both recruited into British secret service and evicted from Italy with the caution to never return. How then does this wicked, worldly wildling make it into the pages of a book on New Hampshire history? Believe it or not, after traveling the globe, starting his own religion and rocking the sensibilities of the Progressive Age, Aleister Crowley decided it was time to move to the tiny village of Hebron, New Hampshire, and retire.

There was, you can probably guess, a woman involved but likely not in the way you're expecting. Evangeline Adams, sometimes described as America's first astrological superstar, was a coauthor of some of Crowley's work and owned a small white clapboard house in Hebron. She, too, was facing a retirement of sorts. Related to two former American presidents, Adams had the pedigree needed to bill herself out as an astrologer to the bluebloods of New York City's wealthy elite. However, Adams had rather famously been arrested for fortunetelling in New York City a number of times. She was acquitted of the charges when she gave the judge an accurate reading of his son based solely on the child's birth date. Nevertheless, Adams had a lot of reasons to believe that she might not be so lucky the next time. She ran her astrology consulting business by mail, often with Crowley's help, and moved to the lakes region of New Hampshire for a change of pace and to extradite herself from the watchful eyes of the New York City Police. Even though the friendship between Adams and Crowley ultimately ended up in court with each accusing the other of taking credit for their own work, in 1916, the two were still as thick as thieves. Crowley followed Adams to New Hampshire and went into what he called his "magickal retirement."

Magickal retirement is a little different than most people's non-magickal retirement, it seems. Crowley didn't take up golf or spend his days lounging on Weirs Beach. Crowley dedicated four months of his New Hampshire life to experimenting with various spooky, secret, arcane

The white clapboard house in Hebron, where Aleister Crowley and his astrologer collaborator retired. *Photo by Renee Mallett.*

The cemetery that sits behind the house where Aleister Crowley spent his magickal retirement. *Photo by Renee Mallett.*

things. The Granite State and his adventures on the shores of Newfound Lake make an appearance in his book *The Confessions of Aleister Crowley*. In the book, Crowley describes taking a potion that gave him superhuman strength and an utter inability to sit still. While under the effects of this magic brew, Crowley said he drew a crowd awed by his uncanny strength while chopping down a tree. Once the unnamed potion wore off, Crowley crucified a toad. This was not meant to be an act of animal cruelty, though the toad may have disagreed. The ritualistic crucifixion resulted in a new friendship for Crowley. "The result was immediately apparent. A girl of the village, three miles away, asked me to employ her as my secretary. I had had no intention of doing any literary work; but as soon as I set eyes on her I recognized that she had been sent for a purpose, for she exactly resembled the aforesaid toad."

The girl began visiting the cottage in Hebron each morning to take dictation for Crowley. Presumably, it was her hand that typed the letter to the *New York Times* in which Crowley described a foot-wide ball of lightning that appeared near his foot inside the New Hampshire cottage during a storm. Crowley also encountered a strange entity in Hebron known as Lam, which some speculate could be an alien. But neither the Live Free or Die state nor the aliens could hold Crowley in one spot for too long. He soon went back to his world-hopping ways—and the court case with Adams. He died on December 1, 1947. The house in Hebron, on the other hand, still stands proudly next door to a classic, steepled church and just in front of a small graveyard, perfectly befitting the place where the wickedest man in the world once retired.

13

PEYTON PLACE

he public loves to create a hero….Sometimes I think they do it for the sheer joy of knocking him down from the highest peak. Like a child who builds a house of blocks and then destroys it with one vicious kick." So says Grace Metalious in *Peyton Place*, the novel that would bring her fame, fortune and a great deal of grief. Her neighbors in Gilmanton, New Hampshire, would probably disagree and say the grief was all theirs.

Peyton Place's author was born Grace DeRepentigny in Manchester, New Hampshire, in 1924. Her prowess as a storyteller made itself known at an early age. Family members remember her even as a young child sitting on a special stool at her grandmother's and spending hours writing. In high school, she would tell classmates her middle name was Marie Antionette, an out-and-out fabrication, and gleefully spread rumors about herself. Her stories raised some eyebrows, even at this early time. In high school, she wrote a play for her local church group that was just questionable enough to cause the priest to refuse to attend but not quite outlandish enough to get the entire production canceled.

Grace married right after graduation and quickly had three children. Her husband, George, was a teacher. But Grace was no typical housewife of her day. Writing still held all of her attention. She would sometimes lock the kids out of the house when the muse called to her. Neighbors clucked their tongues over her lack of care of the house and the washing. The young family soon moved to Gilmanton, but the change of ZIP code did nothing to change Grace's ways. The rented house, which Grace Metalious dubbed "It'll Do," had a well that continually ran dry. Grace didn't care—all the more reason to skip the washing and laundry. It was while living in It'll Do in Gilmanton that Grace got the news that her book *Peyton Place* had been accepted for publication. Friends would say it was the last time they saw the author truly happy.

It was a small publisher, and only a limited release was expected. Grace didn't care. This was what she had been working toward and dreaming of all these years. Alan Brandt, the publicist assigned to the novel, had higher hopes for *Peyton Place* than even its writer. Brandt convinced the publisher to increase his marketing budget and then headed to New Hampshire to see what ideas he could come up with. It was while he was visiting Grace at It'll Do that inspiration struck.

Grace's husband, George, had recently been hired as a principal for one of the local Gilmanton schools. Some residents didn't care for the appointment and tried to get him fired. Grace, alluding to the hullabaloo, mentioned to Alan Brandt that she thought her novel would get George fired for good. By the next day, Brandt had newspapers all over New England writing about the forthcoming novel that was so scandalizing it would jeopardize the employment of the author's husband. The story went national, and *Peyton Place* wound up on the 1956 best-seller lists before it even hit the bookstores. Everyone wanted to read for themselves what a woman could possibly write that would be so unseemly that her husband could lose his job over it.

The rest, as they say, is history. *Peyton Place* stayed at the top of the best-seller lists for two years; has sold more than ten million copies worldwide; and spawned a sequel, a television series and two movies. But the success of the book did nothing to thaw Grace's Gilmanton neighbors' feelings toward her. It actually made relations with the townsfolk worse. With its racy passages; its exposé of small-town life; and a plot that circled around murder, incest and suicide, it was definitely not what people expected a housewife to write. Even Grace's own publisher had dubbed her "Pandora in blue jeans." When the *Peyton Place* movie premiered in Camden, Maine, the movie studio offered twenty-five Gilmanton residents the chance for an all-expenses-paid trip to attend. Only thirteen decided to go. The film went on to receive nine Academy Award nominations.

It didn't help that the media had descended on the small town in full force. No matter how often Grace said the story was not set in Gilmanton, people just refused to believe it. Rumors swirled that certain characters were based on people in town who Grace didn't care for. The book had shattered many

Grace Metalious required that the premiere of *Return to Peyton Place*, the sequel to her best-selling book, which became a movie, would take place at the Colonial Theater in Laconia, New Hampshire. *Photo by Renee Mallett.*

Grace's dream home became the Gilmanton Winery after her death. The winery loves its association with the *Peyton Place* author. *Photo by Renee Mallett.*

illusions about small towns and the people who lived in them. Now readers and reporters all wanted to get a look at the "real" Peyton Place.

Although painfully shy and dreading the media attention, Grace Metalious was, for the first time in her life, really living it up. She bought her dream house, the current location of the Gilmanton Winery and Vineyard, and started a more-or-less nonstop party. Her husband didn't have to worry about how Grace's behavior could affect his job—she divorced him and quickly married a radio personality from Laconia. They lived, if not the good life, at least the wild life, until the *Peyton Place* money couldn't keep up with them. Grace penned a sequel to *Peyton Place* and two other novels, but they never quite lived up to the success of her first novel.

For all of the tongue clucking surrounding *Peyton Place*, what many missed was that it was based on a true crime story that happened right here in New Hampshire. In 1946, a twenty-year-old woman named Barbara Roberts shot and killed her father. With the help of her younger brother, Roberts buried the body beneath the pigpen in the family barn. It remained hidden for eight months. Eventually, two older brothers, merchant marines, came home to find out why they hadn't been receiving any letters from their father. They discovered the grisly crime and turned Barbara in to the authorities. Eventually, she pled guilty to manslaughter and received a five-year prison sentence. The younger brother who helped her conceal the crime also pled guilty and got four years' probation. Barbara had good reason to kill her father, though. He had been sexually abusing her for years. The night of the murder he had snapped and nearly killed her and her younger brother. Grace's publisher was willing to take a risk with some aspects of the story, but some, even coming from real life, were deemed too much for readers' sensitivities. For all of the uproar over Grace's "smutty" book, it had actually been sanitized from some of the worst of the true-to-life occurrences.

Drinking daily took its toll on Grace and all of her relationships. Her second husband left at about the same time the bank accounts started to get low. Grace tried buying a hotel and even named it Peyton Place, but the venture never quite panned out. When she died on February 25, 1965, she was just thirty-nine years old, and her estate was valued at $44,000. She also left an unpaid tax bill for $114,000. Before her death, Grace had bought herself a plot in the Smith Meetinghouse Cemetery in Gilmanton. She also purchased all of the plots surrounding hers so that she could keep herself away from the rest of Gilmanton's residents, even in death.

The cemetery in Gilmanton, where Grace Metalious is buried. *Photo by Renee Mallett.*

Left: Grace's tombstone sits in its own corner of the cemetery. She bought all of the plots surrounding her own to keep her grave separate from the neighbors who dogged her in life. *Photo by Renee Mallett.*

Right: Coins, some from foreign fans, are still left on Grace Metalious's tombstone to this day as a sign of respect. *Photo by Renee Mallett.*

The white stone sits in its own back corner of the graveyard and attracts the curious even today. A friend of Grace's keeps some red flowers at the gravesite and washes the stone regularly. It is common to find loose coins scattered across the top of the stone. They are left as signs of respect and well wishes for the woman who shrugged off criticisms of her best-selling novel by saying, "If I'm a lousy writer, then an awful lot of people have lousy taste.

14

J.D. SALINGER

*G*race Metalious is, of course, not the only author to grace the ranks of residents of the Granite State. In fact, for a relatively small state with just upward of 1.3 million residents, New Hampshire is lousy with writers. Jodi Picoult, Robert Frost, the poet Donald Hall, Dan Brown of *Da Vinci Code* fame, John Irving and Joe Hill—who has won an Eisner Award, a World Fantasy Award, a Bram Stoker Award and a British Fantasy Award for his best-selling books—have all had ties to the Granite State at one point or another. Of course, if you're talking authors and New Hampshire, you have to mention J.D. Salinger.

The *Catcher in the Rye* author was raised in Manhattan, but he chose to spend nearly all of his adult life in Cornish, New Hampshire. J.D. Salinger moved there in 1953, just two years after publishing *Catcher in the Rye*. The book, still read to this day, was a blockbuster right from the start. However, his first home was not. Described by New Hampshire Public Radio as a "falling down barn…no bathroom. No heat," Salinger's first house in Cornish was not what most would have expected for the toast of the literary world. Eventually, he built a second home directly behind this first one that was still modest but at least had heat. He lived there for the rest of his days.

Catcher in the Rye was as much a sensation as Grace Metalious's *Peyton Place*, though the former was critically acclaimed, and the latter raised more eyebrows than literary standards. Though no one is certain why Salinger gave up the limelight to move to the woods of New Hampshire, many have said it was all of the attention that *Catcher in the Rye* brought him. Like Grace

Metalious, Salinger wanted to write books, not give interviews to reporters who insisted his famous *Catcher* main character, Holden Caulfield, was really a stand-in for himself.

Many like to say that Salinger was a recluse during his New Hampshire life. The people of Cornish would take exception to that. The famous author was a fixture in town. It wasn't that he didn't want to see anyone. He just wanted the media and fans to leave him alone. And, luckily for him, the residents of Cornish decided to help him. Fans and reporters often asked around, looking for the reluctant literary star, but residents would profess not to know him. For sixty years, J.D. Salinger lived this way, probably still writing in private but never publishing new works, until his death on January 27, 2010.

15

THE HANGING OF RUTH BLAY

They came just after sunrise, two men and a hard-faced woman. As she was the daughter of a seamstress, the silk gown the woman handed Ruth to wear was not the finest gown she had ever seen, but it might have been the nicest the former schoolteacher had ever worn herself. She put it on slowly under the watchful eye of the woman. Ruth was tired, having spent the evening before under the watch of these same people, writing out a final statement to be published after her death—yes, death.

The fine silk gown was given to Ruth Blay to wear to her execution, as was the custom in the eighteenth century. For the past five months, after a trial that electrified all of New England, Ruth had lived in this squalid jail waiting to be hanged. Three reprieves had previously come down from the governor, holding off the hangman's noose for a time, and it must be assumed that Ruth Blay hoped that the same would happen again.

Ruth Blay was not the typical criminal of the time. The youngest of five sisters, she was raised by a widowed mother from around the year 1743, when Ruth would have been near the age of three. Her mother, Lydia, came from a good family and, by taking in sewing work and marrying off the daughters old enough to leave home, was able to hang on to her home for many years after being widowed.

Ruth Blay came from an educated family. Copies of documents from the time show that William Blay, the father who had died when Ruth was a child, signed his own name with a smooth and practiced hand. Education remained an important part of the children's raising, even as conditions became harder and harder on the Blay homestead. Lydia Blay still found time to pass her knowledge on to Ruth, enough so that the girl would go on to earn her keep as a dame teacher.

In the 1700s, not every town had a school, and not every child had the chance to learn, even if the town did have a school. Dame schools fulfilled an important role in bridging the gap for towns and families that wanted their children to be educated but still home often enough to help. A dame school at this time in New England would only be opened by an at least moderately educated woman, usually in her own home or perhaps a church. It would operate like something between a daycare and a private school. The dame teacher who ran the school would teach both girls and boys the basics of reading and math. Oftentimes, girls were given additional instruction in what would have been considered "womanly" arts—embroidery, needlepoint and sewing. Boys' education would have centered on what they would need to run a family farm or business. Much of the reading taught to girls would have been faith-based, as women were tasked with the moral upbringing of the children who they were expected to one day have.

As a literate daughter of a seamstress, Ruth Blay would have been ideally suited for this type of work. Remaining records from the time seem to indicate that Ruth worked in such a position at one of the nine dame schools found in Chester, New Hampshire. As best as can be determined, Ruth moved in with an older, married sister, Mary Blaisdel, while she worked in the town's dame school. Chester town records show a payment made to the Blaisdel family for boarding schoolteachers, and the surrounding towns of Sandown and Hawke (now Danville) show a Ruth Blay on the payroll of different dame schools as a teacher. They were rural communities with no schools of their own, so it would have been common for Ruth Blay to teach in all of the towns on a rotating basis, working for a few months in Hawke before moving on to Chester's children and then off to Sandown before going back to Hawke and starting the whole thing over again. The children would get a few weeks' worth of lessons in reading and math and then have a few months to pick crops or do any number of other chores on their family farms.

Between the years of 1752 and 1767, we know little of Ruth Blay beyond these few small mentions of payments. Hundreds of young women of her time lived in a similar fashion and have faded into obscurity. In the normal course of events, Blay would have eventually married a young man, probably from the same station of life as herself, and disappeared from the records and minds of historians. However, Ruth Blay's life did not follow the prescribed path dictated by her economic status and the times. Sometime in the fall of 1767, the now thirty-one-year-old dame teacher found herself unmarried and pregnant. This news would not have been as shocking as we might think it was for the time. Historians today believe as many as 40 percent of brides during the pre-Revolutionary time period were probably already expecting when they walked down the aisle.

But marriage was, for some reason, not in the books for Ruth Blay. There was no hasty trip down the aisle to legitimize the child before it was born. On top of this, it would have been nearly impossible for her to keep her position as a dame teacher while being an unmarried mother. Teachers were expected to set an example for the children and to elevate their moral upbringing as much as their ability to do arithmetic. A single mother, by the norms of the time, could do neither.

It's ironic that Ruth's education was, in this case, her undoing. A less educated woman, a poorer woman, a woman from a different kind of family or occupation, could and did get pregnant quite often with little more than spurring on some gossip among neighbors. Ruth did not have the same luxury. She also didn't have the luxury of options. She could name the father before witnesses, particularly during the birthing itself, which might sway the courts into forcing him to help to support her and the baby. But this was not a certain route. If the man was wealthy or well thought of in the community, he would probably be believed over a woman who had already tarnished her own reputation by getting pregnant. If she was believed, the father, and Ruth herself, would face a whipping for fornication. If he was a married man, there would be a charge of adultery on top of that. Some herbs could cause an abortion, but the same herbs in a slightly different dosage might cause Blay's own death at the same time. Adoption was possible if Blay could find a childless couple who would be willing to take the baby in and not name her as the birth mother.

Ultimately, we don't know what Ruth planned to do with the child or why she would not name the father of the baby. Ruth retreated to the South Hampton home of the Currier family around the same time that the pregnancy would have begun to show. During the fall and winter, her belly would have been small and the heavy layers she wore to keep warm would have helped her conceal the pregnancy. But now it was spring. Maternity clothes were rare, and undoubtably, Ruth would not want to call attention to her predicament by buying or wearing any. The woman, skilled in domestic arts, probably loosened the stays in her corsets and widened her underskirts and hoped to pass herself off as simply putting on weight and not as being with child.

On June 10, 1768, Ruth, probably completely alone, gave birth. In later court testimony, she said she had fallen a few days before, felt no movement from the child since that time and then gave birth prematurely to a stillborn daughter. Perhaps in shock and perhaps still trying to conceal the pregnancy, she then hid the infant's body beneath a loose floorboard in the barn where she gave birth.

All of this would be nothing more than a tragic, if not too terribly uncommon, part of Ruth Blay's personal history if not for the fact that four days after the birth of the stillborn baby, a visiting girl discovered the infant's body beneath the barn's floorboards. An investigation was immediately launched, and the very same day, a warrant for Ruth Blay's arrest was issued in South Hampton.

Samuel Folsom, the local coroner, gathered sixteen of the most respected men in the community. This all-male jury, with no legal or medical training among them, were tasked with deciding if the baby was in fact stillborn as Ruth had claimed, which would mean the teacher was just a fornicator, or if the child had been born alive and she was a murderer to boot. Shortly after gathering, they presented the following document with all of their signatures:

Inquisition on the body of a Child supposed of Ruth Blay
An inquisition indented taken at South Hampton June 14, 1768

Within the said province of New Hampshire the fourteenth day of June in the eighth year of his Majesty's Reign King George the Third by the grace of God of Great Britain France and Ireland King Defender of the faith etc. before Samuel Folsom Esq. Coroner of our said Lord the King within the province aforesaid upon the view of the body of a female child then and there being dead by the oath of Benjamin Clough, Samuel Fifield, William Rowell, Joseph Eastman, Moses French, Jeremiah Currier, Samuel Quimbe, Prince Flanders, Moses Hoyt, Stephen Rogers, John Tappan, Onesiphorus Page, James French, Rueben Currier, John Morrill and William Graves, good and lawful men of South Hampton aforesaid within the province aforesaid who being charged and sworn to enquire for our lord the King when & by what means & how the said child came to its death, upon their oath, do say that on the fourteenth day of this instant June one thousand seven hundred and sixty-eight the said child was found dead in the barn of one Benjamin Clough of the aforesd

South Hampton supposed to be born of the body of one Ruth Blay in the said town and it appears to us of the jury that the child came to its death by violence.

Abiah Cooper, a local midwife, was called to complete an examination of Ruth Blay. Cooper was able to confirm that Ruth had recently given birth. Soon after, another doctor was summoned. The effects of giving birth alone, crushing grief and the stress from concealing the body must have been catching up to Ruth, as she was near death herself. The doctor would have to get her on the mend before she could be transported to Portsmouth for trial. It took thirty-five days before the doctor declared her well enough to travel.

The prison in Portsmouth stood roughly where the Music Hall can be found today. It was a two-story building with ten-inch-thick walls and roughly hewn iron bars lining the windows. In the winter, it was frigidly cold. In the summer months, it was hotter than an oven. Ruth spent the next five and a half months here.

Her trial began on September 21, 1768. Witnesses, including Ruth's mother and at least one of her sisters, came before a jury of twelve men to offer what testimony they could in the sorry case. The trial lasted eight hours. The next day, the jury announced that they found Ruth Blay guilty of the crime of the burial and the concealment of her bastard child. The sentence was then passed. Ruth was condemned to hang.

November 24 was declared her execution date. An appeal was not an option in eighteenth-century court cases. But Ruth could, and did, ask for more time to prepare herself mentally and spiritually for death. On November 23, Governor John Wentworth, the son of Benning Wentworth, granted Ruth Blay her first reprieve. She was given two weeks to make herself right with God. Ruth spent the two weeks pleading for more time.

And once again more time was granted. The original execution date had been for November 24, which was then pushed to December 8 and finally to December 24. Once again, another reprieve was asked for and granted, with an execution date of December 30.

On the last night of her life, Ruth wasn't trying to make her peace. She requested a pen and paper so she could write her final witnessed statement about the death of her child. While the full text would be printed in papers across the country the next day under the headline that it was the final *confession* of Ruth Blay, in the letter, she confesses to nothing, calling herself innocent and accusing some for bearing false witness against her:

The Declaration and Confession of Ruth Blay, who was tried at His Majesty's Superior Court in Portsmouth, New Hampshire, September 21, 1768, for concealing the birth of her infant, which was found dead, and is to be executed this 30th day of December 1768.

To the Public,

As it is now but a few Hours, before I must exchange this mortal state, for one that is eternal, it will be no Advantage to me to say any Thing that is amusing, trifling, or impertinent, to the numerous Spectators, some of whom no Doubt, will come out of Curiosity to see the Behavior of the poor condemn'd Person; others out of Pity and Compassion; but whatever may be their View, I now appear a Spectacle to Angels and Men; but what are all things of a temporal Nature to me?—Nothing but God in Christ, and my own Conscience are of any Avail with me;—As to my Fellow Creatures, we are all upon a Level as to the Mercy of God;—they must soon follow, though perhaps not in the same ignominious Way: but the Death I am to undergo, is not so painful as that my Savior has undergone before, on whose merits alone I rely for Pardon and Acceptance—Not but a Consciousness of my own Innocence and his Presence has upheld my drooping Spirits for about five Months, while I have been bound in Chains—It is now needless for me to give a short History of my Life, which I had some Thought of, and perhaps had I done it, though it might seem vain in me, would have appeared as circumspect as some of my Accusers, who have born FALSE WITNESS against me.

Before I enter upon any particulars relating to my Trial and Commendation; I would return my most sincere Thanks to his Excellency the GOVERNOR, for the Reprieves He has already given me from Time to Time; and also to the Reverend MINISTERS, who have so often visited me in my Confinement; and also to their good Offices in a more public Way for my Spiritual Advantage,—And am also far from Casting any Reflection on the honorable JUDGES; as I apprehend the Infatuation must lie in some of the Witnesses, and some of the Jury;—

And now for the Truth of what I am going to say, I appeal to the God before whom I must shortly appear, and call Heaven and Earth to Witness, that though I was with Child, I never had a Single Thought of murdering the Infant, which makes me even shudder to think that it was possible any Mother should be guilty of such Cruelty—and therefore I made Preparation for its Birth, and could now produce the Cloaths and Woman in whose keeping they are; but alas! It is too late;—and on that unhappy Day when I was delivered, I knew that it had not been eight Months from the Time I was with Child, therefore had not Thoughts of being delivered at that time; but an unhappy Fall which I then received, brought on the Birth instantly:—

Having also had another unhappy Fall about ten Days before, which gave me great Uneasiness; and at which Time I apprehend my Child died; so that the Child was dead born: and to conceal the Shame, I hid it in the best Manner I could, and ever after was loath to reveal it, as I imagined no Good could come thereby; but should I have disclosed the whole to my Lawyers, but was advised by my Friends not to do it, and thus I have been condemned.—I must declare to the last that the Witnesses have misinterpreted the Facts, and some of them appeared with Countenances that plainly shewed they were unaffected with the Solemnity of the Trial, and fear they as little regarded the Solemnity of the Oath.—The Time being now so short, after returning Thanks to all Friends for the Kindnesses shown me, I must bid them farewell, and hope that no one will cast any Reflections on my aged Mother, Sisters, and other Relations on my Account, as my Conscience is clear with respect to my Infant;—And although I die with a forgiving Spirit as to all my Enemies, but charge the two Women in particular to examine their own Hearts, as they will answer it another Day, whether they do not come under the Character of false Witnesses?—And whether Prejudice, Jealousy or something else has not drove them thus to bear false Witness against me.

Ruth Blay
PORTSMOUTH PRISON
December 29th, 1768
Thursday Evening eight o'Clock

The foregoing Declaration was read and signed in the presence of three Witnesses and was desir'd
It might be made public immediately.

Though it seems bizarre that Ruth Blay would bother to talk about the clothing she had put aside for this stillborn baby in what would be her final chance to address the charges laid against her, it was actually a very calculating move on the condemned woman's part. Just as, legally, she could have named the father by declaring his name during the birthing process, the "benefit of linen" was a legal maneuver that was used to help women who found themselves in the very predicament Blay was in now. When an unmarried woman was accused of infanticide in the eighteenth century, a popular defense was to show that she had prepared for the birth of the child by supplying it with the linens (clothing, diapers, etcetera) it would need once it was born. The logic was that if a woman had prepared for a baby, it showed an intent to keep the baby. It's unclear why Ruth didn't try to use the defense during her trial if a woman holding the infant's linens really could have come forward.

The last-minute linen defense did nothing for Ruth Blay. The next morning, her jailers brought her a clean dress to wear to her execution. A week before, half a foot of snow had fallen on Portsmouth, but the morning of the hanging was milder than most. Ruth was tied at the hands and feet before being loaded onto an open wagon that also carried the roughly hewn pine box in which she would be buried.

She was driven through the streets of Portsmouth and brought to Gallows Hill. The hill still exists today, though it is now covered by the graves of Portsmouth's South Cemetery. In Ruth's time, the land was owned by the church, and the ranks of the city's dead had not swelled enough to warrant burying them there. On a more typical day in Portsmouth, it was used as pastureland.

What the newspapers described as a "vast concourse of people" from all around the surrounding towns came out to see Ruth hanged. She was right—some came out of curiosity and some came for pity. Even in her own time, many were sympathetic to her cause. So many came that the stone

South Cemetery did not exist when Ruth Blay was hanged. In her time, it was the site of Gallows Hill. *Photo by Renee Mallett.*

wall separating Gallows Hill from Farmer Samuel Hall's land next door was destroyed. He would later petition the City of Portsmouth for money to replace it and would be denied.

Ministers would have stood by her side as her neck was placed in the noose. When women were hanged, their dresses were tied tightly around their ankles so that the final plunge and jerking of their bodies wouldn't accidentally expose spectators to anything lewd. Ruth Blay was given a final chance to speak, but contemporary accounts say all she could do was wail miserably.

Later accounts say that Governor Wentworth did grant another reprieve to Ruth Blay. Usually these stories have the declaration coming just minutes after she was hanged. Others place the blame of the executioner's shoulders, saying he hanged her too early in his hurry to get home for lunch. As best as historians can tell, these are modern inventions made up to satisfy the public's unending fascination with the trials of Ruth Blay. Since 1768, Ruth has been the subject of any number of news stories, books and poems. Ruth Blay was the last woman to be hanged in New Hampshire.

16

THE MURDER OF
JOSIE LANGMAID

*M*any seventeen-year-olds skip school from time to time. But Josie Langmaid wasn't the type of seventeen-year-old who commonly would. When the girl didn't show up at Pembroke Academy on October 4, 1875, her teachers assumed the girl was home sick with her younger brother Waldo. It wasn't until Josie never returned home from school that afternoon that her parents and teachers got together and realized just how long the girl had been missing. Josie normally walked to school with her brother, but that morning, he had stayed home. Josie left for school as normal. But where was she now?

A search party numbering upward of one hundred people quickly assembled to look for the missing girl. They spread out in a thin line and started tramping through the woods between the Langmaids' farm and the school. By 9:00 p.m., the call went out—a body had been discovered. But the discovery was even more grisly than was first imagined. While the body was found fairly quickly, it wouldn't be until the next morning that the girl's head was found farther up the road. Also found nearby was a battered and bloodstained wooden club, presumably one of the weapons used against the poor girl.

The local police realized quickly that they were out of their depth. A crime of this nature had never before occurred in Pembroke. A police detective from Boston was called in to help them investigate the murder. Over the next few weeks, nearly half a dozen men were pulled in for questioning and released. It was one of Josie's teachers who finally gave the cops the clue that led them to their first serious suspect.

Miss Belle Lake, a dame teacher at the Pembroke Academy, said she overheard a local man named William Drew catcall Josie on the street shortly before the murder. Josie Langmaid was so incensed to have been accosted in such a way that she threatened to tell her father what Mr. Drew had said to her. William Drew, according to the teacher, told Josie that if she told anyone, he'd murder her and cut her body into little pieces.

Drew had a reputation for being improper with the young ladies in town. He also went through bouts of unemployment and lived in poverty in a squalid cabin in the woods with his wife. It seemed obvious to most people in town that he was the perpetrator of the outrageous murder. Drew barely escaped a lynch mob before the police could lock him behind bars and start to question his involvement.

Investigators soon found this was not the open-and-shut case they had been hoping for. William Drew, like all of the other previous men brought in for questioning, had an alibi for the morning Josie Langmaid was killed. Miss Belle Lake, for reasons she never explained, had lied about the exchange between Drew and the murdered girl.

In the end, it was a telegram from Vermont, not a schoolteacher or Boston detective, that closed the case. Selectmen from St. Albans, Vermont, hearing of Josie Langmaid's brutal murder, were surprised to see obvious parallels to a crime that had occurred in their own town a year before. Marietta Ball, a St. Albans schoolteacher, had been just as brutally murdered. The local police force there were certain that a man named Joseph Lapage had raped and killed the teacher, but they were unable to find the evidence needed to convict him of the crime. Lapage had moved before ever being successfully linked to the gruesome murder.

The Pembroke Police were stunned. They knew Joseph Lapage. He had moved to town just a few months before with his wife and four of their five children. Searching the Lapage home, they found a bloody coat and a pair of boots whose heels perfectly matched a mark that had been left on Josie Langmaid's face when her killer had stepped on her head to steady it as he cut it from the body.

Lapage, like those before him, had an alibi. A popular leader in the local French community, Joe Daniels, told police that Lapage had been with him cutting wood that infamous morning. The problem was that Lapage had already given his statement to the police, and he not only didn't mention that he was chopping wood, but he had given an entirely different story to explain his whereabouts. Lapage had told police that he had no alibi because he had spent that morning lost in the very woods where they had found Josie's body.

On October 28, 1875, Lapage was formally charged with the murder of Josie Langmaid. The trial that followed sealed the case against Lapage. Several witnesses came forward to say they had seen the accused killer on the same road as the school that morning carrying a wooden club. Lapage's sister-in-law testified that he had threatened her with a club and raped her five years before. Lapage was convicted, had his verdict thrown out for a legal technicality and was tried again. This time, the first-degree murder conviction stuck. Lapage was sentenced to hang.

On the day before his March 15, 1878 execution, Lapage confessed to the murders of Josie Langmaid and Marietta Ball. He showed authorities where he had hidden some small possessions he'd taken from Josie after he killed her, laying to rest any questions anyone might have had about his guilt. In one final twist of irony, once Lapage explained the exact route he had taken that morning, it became obvious that all of the witnesses who had testified to seeing him on the street with a club had been lying.

Even after Lapage confessed and was hanged for his crimes, the people of Pembroke still needed a resolution to the crime. A large stone monument was erected in Josie's honor. While it was a nice thought on behalf of the citizens of Pembroke, the marker gives eerily specific directions to the exact locations that both the head and the body of the slain girl were discovered.

The monument to Josie Langmaid is not the only murder monument in New Hampshire. Colebrook, New Hampshire, features its own stone edifice commemorating another senseless crime. In 1997, Carl Drega of Bow, New Hampshire, was pulled over by state police for the offense of driving a rusted-through pickup truck.

Drega shot and killed the officers who had tried to ticket him. Then, deciding he had nothing to lose, Drega stole their police car and drove downtown to shoot Judge Vicki Bunnell. Drega's final victim was Dennis Joos, a newspaper editor who was drawn by the sound of gunfire. He died while trying to wrestle the gun from Drega's hand.

Drega returned home to Bow and burned his own house to the ground. He made it as far as Vermont before police gunned him down. As with the much earlier murder of Josie Langmaid, Colebrook residents had a hard time coming to grips with the crime spree that had suddenly overtaken their small town. They erected a black stone memorial etched with the faces of state troopers Leslie Lord and Scott Philips, Judge Vicki Bunnell and journalist Dennis Joos.

17

THE OVERDUE LIBRARY BOOK

*I*t's a misunderstanding that drinking alcohol was illegal during Prohibition. The Eighteenth Amendment only specifically forbade the manufacture, sale and transport of intoxicating liquors. But the case against alcohol was made in New Hampshire long before the amendment was considered. Even before the Civil War, New Hampshire had tried banning sales of alcohol around the state. The idea was quickly reversed, but that didn't stop Henry Blair, a congressman and later senator from New Hampshire, from introducing legislation outlawing alcohol on a federal level twice. Both times, his efforts failed. In the earliest parts of the nineteenth century, the State of New Hampshire gave local town governments the ability to restrict alcohol consumption outside of a resident's private home. Many towns took this direction to curb alcohol sales.

While the ideas behind Prohibition, what then president Herbert Hoover dubbed the "Noble Experiment," were well intentioned, the practice didn't quite work out the way many had hoped. Overnight, legal business owners were driven out of business, and criminals stood up in their place to satisfy the public's demand for a drink. Costs to municipalities skyrocketed with the tax income from alcohol sales suddenly gone and the criminal justice budget rising. Instead of cutting down on death and crime, Prohibition increased it.

The alcohol that did manage to get transported into the United States during this time was often watered down to increase profits. Creosote, a carcinogen that is normally used as a wood preservative, was added to deepen the color of the watered-down brews. Embalming fluid was sometimes added to the mix to give the drink the bite of true alcohol. Three thousand people a year died from tainted liquor they bought from mobsters and bootleggers during Prohibition. The famous mobster Al Capone is thought to have made as much as $60 million selling illegal alcohol using these methods.

The notoriety of the criminals who were cashing in on the Eighteenth Amendment was one of the most frustrating things for law enforcement at that time. It became fashionable to flaunt one's crimes, at least enough to get some street credibility but not enough to get caught. Often, law enforcement knew exactly who was bringing in the alcohol and exactly how they were doing it, but they just couldn't get around the red tape to do what they needed to stop them. In New England, Coast Guard patrols were especially interested in a Canadian boat named *I'm Alone*. They saw the ship often as it made its way from the Caribbean up the coast, always staying just far enough out to sea as to be out of the Coast Guard's reach.

The large schooner could carry as much as 2,800 cases of liquor when it was full. The boat would sit safely out in international waters and let the bootleggers and rumrunners take all the risk in coming up to it and loading on as much alcohol as they could carry. *I'm Alone* was the most famous of these ships, picking up alcohol in the Caribbean and supplying most of the East Coast, but it was not, as its name implied, alone in these endeavors. Any number of ships were using the same methods to sneak in as much alcohol as they could get past the cops.

Every Coast Guard ship in the country was on the lookout for the chance to apprehend *I'm Alone*. And in the winter of 1928, a cutter named the *Wolcott* got its chance.

Dumb luck led the *Wolcott* into the path of *I'm Alone* off the coast of Louisiana. The *Wolcott*'s captain requested permission to board *I'm Alone*. Unsurprisingly, that ship's captain declined. An argument followed with the *I'm Alone* insisting it was fourteen miles out to sea and therefore in international waters. The Coast Guard insisted just as urgently that the boat was only ten miles out and therefore in its jurisdiction. After a two-day standoff, a second Coast Guard ship arrived to back up the *Wolcott*. The message was made clear—*I'm Alone* would allow the Coast Guard to board or they would sink the ship.

I'm Alone chose to fight. Faced with two Coast Guard ships, it was a risky choice. In a very short amount of time, the hull of *I'm Alone* was breached, and the entire ship sank beneath the waves of the deep blue sea. The Coast Guard rescued all but one of the *I'm Alone* crew and headed back into port, ready for the accolades that would come with finally getting the most infamous of the bootleggers' fleet.

Instead, they returned to find themselves embroiled in an international controversy. *I'm Alone* was registered in Canada, and that country declared the Coast Guard had no right to sink one of its ships. Any evidence of rumrunning had sunk along with the ship. Suddenly, the United States saw itself not only having to apologize for sinking the criminal boat but also having to pay for it.

The United States scrambled to save face—and the $386,000 Canada said it was owed for the sinking of the ship. The U.S. government decided the entire mess could be resolved if only it could show that Americans owned the boat even though it was registered in Canada. Investigators were sent to find out everything they could about the submerged schooner.

There wasn't much to find. The Coast Guard had never come close to catching *I'm Alone*. It had, however, just a few short months before the sinking, nearly caught one of the smaller ships that carried the contraband liquor from *I'm Alone* to the shore. A Coast Guard cutter had nearly caught the *Cheri* when the crew of that ship torched the boat and jumped overboard, hoping to destroy any evidence that might be used against them. At the time, they had succeeded. By the time the Coast Guard had been able to board the burned-out wreck of the *Cheri*, all that remained was a single charred library book.

It was this book that investigators turned to now, hoping that some overlooked clue might help the government out of the mess it currently found itself in. The book was from the Portsmouth library and still stamped on the card was the name of the man who had borrowed it so many months before. Danny Hogan proved to be a valuable source of information on the ownership of *I'm Alone*. Armed with the name of one of the crew, the Coast Guard made quick work of untangling the provenance of *I'm Alone*. Danny Hogan, American enough to have qualified for a New Hampshire library card, had bought the boat along with two of his gangster friends several months before the sinking. Suddenly, the conversation between the United States and Canada shifted. Ultimately, the United States paid some damages for the sinking of the ship, but it was nowhere near the lofty sum first tossed around, and Danny Hogan and his friends were convicted of transporting alcohol.

18

MADAME SHERRI

*E*ven today, more than fifty years after her death, people love to share gossip about Madame Sherri. Some local favorites have the jazz-era icon being driven around Chesterfield, New Hampshire, wearing her famous fur coat—and nothing else—and running a swanky brothel frequented by mobsters and Supreme Court justices.

Of course, a great many of these stories are just as fictitious as the flapper's name. That's right, like many of the other people mentioned in this book, Madame Sherri is famous under a name not her own. When she was born in 1878 in Paris, her parents named her Antoinette Bramare. She'd grow up to be a seamstress, working on the Parisienne shows. In later years, she skewed this fact into fanciful tales of being one of the biggest names in European theater and not a simple costumer for the theater.

In 1909, Madame Sherri, the legend, got its start. Antoinette met Anthony Macaluso. Macaluso was traveling under the name Andre Reila because, well, quite simply, he was a wanted man. Macaluso had been indicted in a rather famous blackmail scheme just a few years before. Fleeing to Europe, Macaluso was looking to keep his freedom—not to fall in love. But shortly after meeting Antionette, the two married and made plans to return to the United States, the very country from which Macaluso had fled.

The young couple made their way to New York on one of the lavish transatlantic steamships run by the White Star Line of *Titanic* infamy. They opened a posh millinery on Forty-Second Street. But making hats was not nearly how the two wanted to make their names. Both had a true passion

The remains of the curved staircase at Madame Sherri's Forest. *Photo by Renee Mallett.*

for the theater—and for the money and celebrity that swirled around it. Antoinette's years as a seamstress were put to good use creating fantastical costumes for Broadway shows.

Eventually, though, Macaluso's dark past caught up to them. In a surprise twist of fate, it happened when the couple was robbed. Macaluso reported a large theft to the New York City Police, saying that a serving girl had stolen $30,000 worth of jewels from his wife. As luck would have it, the very detective assigned to the case of the stolen jewels happened to be one who had worked Macaluso's blackmail attempt from years earlier. Shortly after meeting the supposed Andre Reila, the detective put two and two together and realized who he had really been speaking to. Macaluso was arrested on the spot. However, Macaluso proved adept at evading justice. Shortly after being released on bail, charges against him were dropped due to lack of evidence.

Perhaps trying to shed the last of this felonious history from their lives and perhaps just looking to add a little flash to their business, Antoinette Bramare adopted the Sherri name. For the next eight years, she would design Broadway wardrobes and dancing costumes for the Ziegfeld Follies. Macaluso gained some small fame as a dancer on the vaudeville circuit. But the couple's turn to a legitimate life was not unmarred by scandal. In 1924,

Macaluso went blind and insane from venereal disease before dying at the Manhattan State Hospital.

Now a widow, Madame Sherri quickly took up a relationship with a stage actor named Jack Henderson who was as famous for the titillating parties he threw up north in his New Hampshire home as he was for acting. The wild parties were just what Sherri needed to get over the death of her husband. When seventy acres of land and a small farmhouse, immediately adjacent to Henderson's parcel, went up for sale in Chesterfield, Madame Sherri snatched it up. Over the next few years, she bought more and more adjoining lots, until, ultimately, she had over six hundred acres to call her own.

After acquiring the acreage, Madame Sherri started work on a house that was something both more and less than a home. Her descent into eccentricity now well started, Sherri designed all aspects of the house herself. She did so with no formal training, no blueprint and no real idea of how a house should be built. Stories from the time tell of her tripping over woodland in a pair of ridiculous high heels better suited for shopping in Manhattan than hiking, dropping pegs as she went and describing her vision to the perplexed carpenters she had brought in to build her dream home. Ultimately, they did their best to form her vision into a working house. It was a three-story

How Madame Sherri's castle looked shortly after being built. *Library of Congress public domain.*

monstrosity that her baffled Chesterfield neighbors would quickly dub the "castle." Partially inspired by Roman architecture, partially modeled after a French chalet, the castle featured a basement bistro, trees growing through the bar that took up the entire first floor and an enormous stone staircase that ran up the side of the house to private apartments above.

This was not a house for living. Madame Sherri still lived in the modest farmhouse she had originally bought across the road. The castle was kept aside specifically for partying. And the parties at Madame Sherri's nearly didn't stop. She held court in an enormous cobra-shaped chair that was more of a throne than a mere piece of furniture. People said she smoked so constantly that she only had to light one cigarette a day and could keep the rest going from the smoking ashes of the previous one.

Madame Sherri kept a small monkey on a gold leash. She was never without a wad of bills secured in the plunging cleavage of her dress. Her extravagance knew no bounds. Of course, her Chesterfield neighbors had to wonder where on earth she got all of her money. Madame Sherri said she was a famed European actress, but even in the woods of New Hampshire, enough people knew better. This is when the rumors of brothels and mobsters started up, trying to explain Madame Sherri's seemingly limitless wealth.

Each year sees new degradation to the remains of the great stone staircase at Madame Sherri's. *Photo by Renee Mallett.*

Right: The stone fireplace was one of the few things to survive the blaze that left the castle in ruins. *Photo by Renee Mallett.*

Below: The stone foundations also survived the fire that took the rest of the structure. *Photo by Renee Mallett.*

These stone stairs once led to Madame Sherri's private apartment above the castle, though she lived directly across the street. *Photo by Renee Mallett.*

Madame Sherri's Forest is a popular spot for hiking. Most people stop to take photos of the castle ruins. *Photo by Renee Mallett.*

But the truth is that Madame Sherri had been living well beyond her means for many, many years. The constant entertaining ate up whatever money the building of the house hadn't burned through. Suddenly, Sherri needed to scheme to even keep the land she had so furiously collected years earlier. Thinking that partying had gotten her into this mess and could maybe get her out of it, Madame Sherri turned the castle into a nightclub. When attendees realized they wouldn't be having the same star-studded events that Sherri had been famous for in her personal life, the scheme failed quickly.

Then, in a sudden about-turn, Madame Sherri found God. She became a Jehovah's Witness and moved to Vermont. The conversion didn't stick, though. Within six months, she had returned to Chesterfield and the castle.

Or, it might be better to say she returned to the remains of the castle. In the few short months she was gone, the property had been raided and all but destroyed. The fine throne she had sat on for years had been stolen to be used as a prom night prop at the local high school, every window was broken and even the front door had been carted away. Madame Sherri never stepped foot in the castle again after seeing it ruined.

Madame Sherri lived to be eighty-four years old but died in poverty in Brattleboro, Vermont, in 1965. She had fallen so far from her glamorous

These stairs wrapped around the far side of the castle in Madame Sherri's day. *Photo by Renee Mallett.*

life that she died a ward of the state. It's unknown if she was even aware of the fate of her beloved castle. In 1962, all but the curved stone staircase, the fireplace and stone foundation was burned to the ground by vandals, but really, the castle had fallen to ruin even before that final smoking blow.

The stone staircase is still an iconic landmark, but where the rich and famous of the theater world once partied is now conservation land. Now 488 acres of land make up what is called Madame Sherri's Forest. A display at the front of the hiking trails gives visitors an overview of what an enigmatic figure Madame Sherri was.

19

THE FROG EATER

Without further ceremony he put his hand in his blouse pocket and pulled out a
frog, live and kicking lustily; took it by the hind legs, threw back his head, opened
his mouth wide as a fly trap, and ushered the frog head first down his throat.
Another, and still another, followed and shared the same fate as the first, until
half a dozen large-sized frogs were hopping around in his stomach together.
—*Alive Frog Eater,* NY Star

*L*ive frog eating is just one of the odd stories attributed to the hermit known as English Jack. It's also one of the few stories known to actually be true. Even his name is up for debate, with local papers and postcards at the time dubbing him English Jack, newspaper interviews calling him everything from Alfred Viell to Viles to Vials and his tombstone declaring itself to mark the final resting place of John Vials.

English Jack was something of a quirky figure beloved by tourists in and around Crawford Notch in the 1870s. There are even some existing travel brochures that mention the hermit as an attraction of sorts to look out for when enjoying the natural beauty of the area. One even attributed the modest age of 110 years to him. Each brochure seemed intent on outdoing the others with outlandish stories of English Jack, and the swindler was happy to let them do it.

The frog eating isn't mentioned in the earliest records of him, but once a Lowell, Massachusetts paper mentioned the strange dietary choice, English Jack began to show up at all sorts of places in the White Mountains with pockets full of amphibians for snacking.

English Jack began to tell the newspapermen who appeared on his doorstep that as a young man he had been a sailor. His penchant for eating frogs, he would say, stemmed from the year he had spent shipwrecked in the Mediterranean. He credited his willingness to eat snakes and frogs for his survival during this disaster. In case the newspapermen weren't forthcoming with a payment for hearing his life story, English Jack would add that he was willing to eat frogs again—if there was a profit in it.

It would be a little unfair to call English Jack a con man. It seems that he did, after all, really eat the frogs. But it's hard to consider him a true hermit when he was walking around town giving interviews and snacking on toads. Soon there were even excursions for tourists to visit him. For a hermit, Jack was quite the showman, selling his homebrewed beer and quipping about how much smarter he was than the very rich who paid one dollar to eat frog legs while he had the entire animal to eat for free.

English Jack the Hermit was a real cottage industry for many years. His hut appeared on postcards and his life story in cheaply produced pamphlets. He even made an appearance in a romanticized poem about his life.

20

THE FIREMAN'S RIOT

*I*t was 1839 when the residents of Manchester voted to create a fire department, with a $1,000 budget and a fire station that was built for just $90. Considering Manchester's long history with devastating fires, the move was probably long overdue. For much of the early history of the city, residents dealt with fires or floods, and the two disasters seemed to rotate regularly.

The newly formed fire department, run primarily by fire wards Amory Warren and Walter French, was certainly kept busy in those early years. In 1840, they battled an enormous fire that completely destroyed the Island Mill located just below the Amoskeag Falls, which left over one hundred employees without jobs. In 1844, the Manchester Town Hall, only three years old at the time, burned to the ground in just one hour, despite the best efforts of everyone involved to save it. Manchester's current town hall sits on the ruins of that original one. In 1850, the top floor of Stark Mill, one of the most prosperous mills in the city, was lost to fire. That prompted the town to start paying its firemen for the first time—a generous five dollars a year plus an extra twenty cents for answering an alarm and forty cents on top of that for every hour worked.

But, ironically, one of the most devastating events in Manchester's history was caused by firemen—not stopped by them. In September 1859, Manchester held a firemen's muster, and 2,500 firemen from around New England came to take part in the festivities. The muster was to be held in Park Square, which most New Hampshirians know today as Veterans

Manchester's city hall is a replacement for an earlier structure that burned down. *Photo by Renee Mallett.*

Park. (The name was changed in 1985.) In 1859, Park Square featured a large pond, which, sadly, no longer exists today. As part of the muster, an enormous firepole, topped by a great gold sculpture, was added to the park just beyond the pond.

That Manchester was selected to host the firemen's muster was an honor to be sure. And business owners expected to rake in a lot of money from the festivities. At this time in the city's history, Manchester was something of a wild town filled with taverns, gambling halls and more than a few shady dealings. The general feeling was that adding a few thousand firemen into the mix would make for a rousing party. Few people stood to make more from the firemen's muster than Nathaniel Perkins. He owned the Washington House, a popular nightspot that was sure to turn a nice profit. But Perkins had some concerns about the city absorbing that many visitors at one time. He was probably one of the loudest opponents of the event.

The first inkling that things might head south started early. People started complaining almost from the start that Manchester was starting to look like a shantytown. Tent villages had sprung up all over the city, and stinking masses of people with no bathroom facilities were at every corner and in every yard and every farmer's field. With every hotel booked solid, the firemen and their families had to stay somewhere.

Even so, things were moving along fairly smoothly until the evening of September 14, 1859. A fireman by the name of Hepburn, visiting from Charlestown, Massachusetts, was drinking and gambling in Underhill's Saloon for most of the night. By all accounts, he was favored by lady luck at the card tables that night. But lady luck wasn't on his side when he went to cash in his chips. Among the piles of bills the cashier passed him there was a very obvious counterfeit five-dollar bill.

For whatever reason, Hepburn didn't call out the cashier in the moment. Instead, he returned to the Faro tables and tried to buy chips with the counterfeit bill. Immediately, and quite rightly, the dealer called him out for the forgery. Hepburn, just as rightly, retorted that the bill had come from the saloon's own cashier. Egged on by alcohol and the hoots and hollers of all assembled, things escalated.

The question of who swung at whom first would become as contentious a question as whether the counterfeit bill was the fault of the saloon or Hepburn. What is for sure is that the dealer was a former prizefighter, and he laid Hepburn out flat.

The visiting firemen instantly put up their fists, outraged at the disrespect shown to their coldcocked brother. The townies were just as quick to defend the dealer, who they considered one of their own. In an instant, a fight broke out that engulfed the entire crowd in Underhill's Saloon. The rowdy little establishment had seen its share of fights over the years but nothing on the scale of what was happening that night. The saloon was quickly destroyed, but the infuriated crowd was just getting started.

Underhill's was located in the basement of a hotel called the Elm House, so the crowd naturally moved upstairs. By the next morning, Elm House was still standing, but it was a gutted shell with only one window left unbroken. Rumors, half-truths and flat-out lies spread fast, and more and more people joined the mob. In a short amount of time, the mob had grown to an all-out riot, smashing windows, overturning anything that could be flipped and lighting fires as they went up the street.

Later estimates were that three hundred gallons of liquor were dumped on the streets as the mob pillaged taverns and added fuel to the blaze. By the next morning, large swaths of the city were destroyed. Nearly every saloon and gambling hall in the city had been reduced to rubble. The only one left standing was the one owned by Nathaniel Perkins. Warned ahead of time that the mob was headed his way, Perkins had met them at the door of the Washington House with a pistol in each hand. In a calm, strong voice he called out over the din that the Washington House was closed for the night and that he would kill any man who tried to enter.

The event would go down as the worst riot in Manchester's history. It had other long-ranging consequences as well. Manchester beefed up its police force and put the new recruits to work raiding the saloons that had quickly been rebuilt after the fire. Nathaniel Perkins was marked by the riot too. He was now known around town as Two Gun Perkins.

21

SUSPECTED WITCHCRAFT

GOODY COLE

Eunice Cole was, admittedly, not the kind of person you would want to have for a neighbor. She was old, disagreeable and possessed the type of temper that caused her contemporaries to describe her as both hated and feared. Goody Cole was a fierce follower of Reverend John Wheelwright, a Puritan clergyman who would be exiled from Massachusetts for his belief in antinomianism, an idea that legal and societal norms could be rejected in place of one's own spiritual code. As you can image, this did not endear Goody Cole to the rest of the population of Hampton, New Hampshire. In Joseph Dow's *History of the Town of Hampton, New Hampshire*, he writes that Goody Cole was said to be "ill-natured and ugly, artful and aggravating, malicious and revengeful."

If Goody Cole was revengeful, history shows that she probably had some good reasons to be. Surviving records show that she was called to court at least a dozen times between the years 1645 and 1656 to defend herself against accusations of slanderous speeches. Many of these documents seem to indicate that she was guilty not of slander but rather of happily voicing unpopular opinions. At times, she had to travel as far south as Boston to answer for something she had said.

In 1656, residents came up with a new kind of charge to use against Goody Cole. Several people stood before the court and accused her of being a witch. As with many of these kinds of accusations, the evidence used against her was nearly impossible to defend against. People told stories of falling sick after drinking from a well on Cole's property. But some of these sicknesses came months after they had quenched their thirst from her well. A neighbor said one of his cows had died and another went missing months after Cole had berated him for letting the cows graze on her land. Other accusations against her included conjuring up a storm on a clear day and causing boats to capsize from great distances.

Unsurprisingly, Goody Cole was convicted. The courts could have executed her for the crime. Instead, they were lenient. She got a public whipping and life imprisonment. But jail couldn't hold Cole for long. She was released, accused again and tried again for the crime of witchcraft three times in her life. Goody Cole holds the odd distinction of being the only woman convicted of witchcraft in New Hampshire.

Each time Cole left prison, she would return to Hampton, to the chagrin of her neighbors. The constant court battles, accusations and time in prison took their toll on her. Each time she came home to Hampton, the conditions

Left: The Tuck Museum not only has information on Goody Cole, but it is also located near her unmarked grave. *Photo by Renee Mallett.*

Right: The Eunice "Goody" Cole monument located near the Tuck Museum. *Photo by Renee Mallett.*

she lived in would get poorer and poorer. When she died in 1680, she was living in a ramshackle shack near the bottom of Rand's Hill near where the Tuck Museum stands today.

Local legend says that when Goody Cole died, the people of Hampton drove a stake through her heart to drive the devil out of her and then placed an iron horseshoe atop her grave. Iron is one of the charms used in folklore to repel witches. The final resting place of Goody Cole is unknown to this day.

If Goody Cole truly loved revenge as much as history tells us she did, then the old witch would probably be pleased with how her story has turned out because it does not end with an unmarked grave in 1680. In 1939, the people of Hampton finally had a change of heart about the disagreeable old lady and voted to exonerate Goody Cole of the crime of witchcraft. As part of the 300th anniversary of the town of Hampton, a group of concerned citizens cleared her name and created a monument in her honor.

JANE WALFORD GETS HER DUE

While Goody Cole was the only woman in New Hampshire to be convicted of witchcraft, it's not for lack of trying. At the same time that Goody Cole was first getting the charge leveled against her, similar accusations were flying around Portsmouth about an equally disliked woman named Jane Walford.

Like Goody Cole, Walford was an outspoken woman of her time. In fact, she had originally tried to settle in Charlestown, Massachusetts, but concerned citizens there had her banished for unorthodox behavior. It turns out that her neighbors in Portsmouth didn't care for her ways any more than those in Charlestown had.

Jane Walford was a healer of some note. But even her caretaking was used against her. Those who lived near the woman testified that she had caused everything from heart palpitations to delusions. In an unusual stroke of luck for Walford, the charges against her were dropped when the judge assigned to her case decided it was an unprovable charge.

The reprieve was short-lived. Like Goody Cole, accusation followed accusation. But in Walford's case, she was never convicted. Jane Walford even managed to have her day in court. In 1669, she took her accusers before the judge and successfully sued for slander. The courts awarded Jane Walford a settlement of five pounds for her trouble.

22

THE MURDER OF JONAS L. PARKER

One of the most sensational crimes in the annals of New Hampshire history has been more or less forgotten to time. While the murder and subsequent trials surrounding Jonas L. Parker were followed by many in their day, few current Granite State residents know the story.

Jonas Parker moved to Manchester with his brother. The former Massachusetts native was drawn to the city in the hopes of making his name and his fortune. And make a name he did, though it was not in the way most people would hope for. In an earlier time in history, if he had been a woman, his neighbors probably would have tried to have him labeled a witch. The man quickly earned a reputation for being an all-around scoundrel. This unfavorable characterization was only reinforced by the ways in which he chose to build his empire—namely taverns, gambling and bowling alleys. Scandalized Manchester residents might not have liked how Mr. Parker chose to make his money, but that didn't stop any of them from flocking to the very establishments they looked down on him for owning. The saloon in particular was a hot spot for the hip upper class of the city.

If people found the disagreeable Mr. Parker suspect from the start, that's nothing compared to what they thought of him once he launched his fledgling political career. Somehow, the unpopular saloon owner, who had just recently moved to the city from Massachusetts, found himself with a choice appointment as Manchester's tax collector. Many at the time speculated that Mr. Parker had blackmailed his wealthy and well-connected bar patrons to get himself the position. It just seemed too big of a pill to swallow. How did this recent transplant who spent his days drinking and gambling in the bar he lived above manage to get such a trusted position in the city government?

Despite considering himself a shrewd businessman, Jonas Parker had other habits that concerned his Manchester neighbors, namely his habit of flashing his money around for all to see. Whether playing cards or walking the streets of the city to collect taxes, Parker never missed the opportunity to open the oversized money purse he carried and pull a big wad of bills from one of the two wallets located within. Since the purse contained all of the daily profit from the bar, the gambling tables and the bowling alley, as well as the tax monies for the town, Parker always had an eye-popping amount of currency on his person at any given time.

It was the evening of March 26, 1845, when fate, or at least his own poor choices, caught up to Mr. Parker. He was in the usual spot in his tavern playing cards when a mysterious man came to the door asking to speak to him privately. The two conferred for a few minutes before Parker opened the till, took out the day's take and hurriedly left with the stranger. It was the last time anyone would see Jonas Parker alive.

His body was found the next morning just a few blocks from the bar in the woods at the outskirts of town. His personal wallet, containing an unknown amount of money, was gone. But the smaller of the two wallets was left untouched and filled with $1,635 of the town's tax dollars. No one could say for certain how much money might have been stolen from Parker's personal purse, but it could have been many times more than the tax dollars that had strangely been left behind.

The trampled remains of winter snow around the body told at least part of the tale of what had occurred the night before. Parker had fought heroically for his life. He was a powerfully built man used to wrestling belligerent drunks at the card tables. He had not been overpowered easily. Next to the body, police found a knife and a straight razor. After being severely beaten, Parker's throat had been slit.

While Parker wasn't well thought of in life, in death the city embraced him and cried out for justice. Though the motive seemed obvious, the crime itself was shocking. Manchester residents demanded a swift conclusion to the case.

They would be left unsatisfied. Ultimately, four men were accused of the crime and four men were acquitted after sensational trials. The murderer of Jonas L. Parker was never found.

BIBLIOGRAPHY

"Aleister Crowley's Magickal Retirement." Atlas Obscura. May 22, 2019. https://www.atlasobscura.com.

Bastoni, Mark. "Isles of Shoals Murders: Horror on Smuttynose Island." *Yankee Magazine*, 1980.

"Benning Wentworth and His Scandalous Marriage." Wentorth Coolidge Mansion. May 23, 2019. https://wentworthcoolidge.org.

Brown, Janice. "Manchester NH: Veterans Park and Monuments" *Cow Hampshire* (blog). May 23, 2014. https://www.cowhampshireblog.com.

Callahan, Michael. "Peyton Place's Real Victim." *Vanity Fair*, January 22, 2007.

Citro, Joseph A. *Curious New England: The Unconventional Traveler's Guide to Eccentric Destinations.* Lebanon, NH: University Press of New England, 2004.

———. *Weird New England: Your Travel Guide to New England's Local Legends and Best Kept Secrets.* New York: Sterling Publishing Company, 2005.

Clayton, John. *You Know You're in New Hampshire When.* Guilford, CT: Globe Pequot Press, 2005.

Daniel, Glyn, "America B.C." *New York Times*, March 13, 1977.

"Desperately Seeking Salinger." *New Hampshire Magazine*, February 28, 2011. https://www.nhmagazine.com.

Duckler, Ray. "That Statue You Often Pass? There's Quite a Story Behind It." *Concord Monitor*, April 14, 2019.

"Face of Old Man on the Mountain in Franconia Notch Fell 15 Years Ago." *Concord Monitor*, April 30, 2018.

Goudsward, David, and Stone, Robert E. *America's Stonehenge: The Mystery Hill Story*. Wellesley, MA: Brandon Books, 2003.

"H.H. Holmes." Biography. Updated August 16, 2019. https://www.biography.com.

"History of the Manchester NH Fire Department: In the Beginning." City of Manchester, New Hampshire. June 6, 2019. http://www.manchesternh.gov.

Hurley, Sean. "Inside J.D. Salinger's House." New Hampshire Public Radio. Updated June 13, 2019. https://www.nhpr.org.

Jones, Eric. *New England Curiosities: Quirky Characters, Roadside Oddities, and Other Offbeat Stuff*. Guilford, CT: Globe Pequot Press, 2006.

"Josie Langmaid Monument." Atlas Obscura. June 1, 2019. https://www.atlasobscura.com.

Kelly, George. "Fifty Shades of Grace." *New Hampshire Magazine*, March 1, 2013.

Larrabee, Eric. "New Hampshire's Own Witch Hunt." New Hampshire Public Radio. June 18, 2005. https://www.nhpr.org.

"Martha Hilton Wentworth Chooses a Husband." New England Historical Society. http://www.newenglandhistoricalsociety.com.

Marvin, Carolyn. *Hanging of Ruth Blay: An Eighteenth-Century New Hampshire Tragedy*. Charleston, SC: The History Press, 2010.

Mayo, Matthew P. *Speaking Ill of the Dead: Jerks in New England History*. Guilford, CT: Globe Pequot Press, 2013.

McCain, Diana Ross. *Mysteries and Legends of New England*. Guilford, CT: Globe Pequot Press, 2009.

Morcom, Richmond. "They All Loved Lucy." *American Heritage* 21, no. 6 (October 1970). https://www.americanheritage.com.

Muise, Peter. "Aleister Crowley's New Hampshire Vacation." *New England Folklore* (blog). August 26, 2012. http://newenglandfolklore.blogspot.com.

"Murder Castle." History. July 13, 2017. https://www.history.com.

Parker, Gail Underwood. *More than Petticoats: Remarkable New Hampshire Women*. Guilford, CT: Morris Book Publishers, 2009.

"Prohibition in New Hampshire: Dream to Nightmare." https://www.alcoholproblemsandsolutions.org.

"Roadside History: Captain Lovewell's War Against the Abenaki." *Union Leader*, October 23, 2016. https://www.unionleader.com.

Robinson, Dennis L. "Lady Wentworth." Seacoast New Hampshire and South Coast Maine. 2005. http://www.seacoastnh.com.

Rogak, Lisa. *Stones and Bones of New England: A Guide to Unusual, Historic, and Otherwise Notable Cemeteries*. Guildford, CT: Globe Pequot Press, 2004.

Rogers, Montana. "The Mystery Stone of Lake Winnipesaukee." New England Today Living. March 22, 2019. https://newengland.com.

"The Scandalous Wedding of Gov. John Wentworth." New England Historical Society. Updated 2019. http://www.newenglandhistoricalsociety.com.

Schechter, Harold. *Depraved*. New York: Simon and Schuster, 2008.

Thorpe, Ashton L. *Manchester of Yesterday*. Manchester, NH: Granite State Press, 1939.

The following websites were helpful in the creation of this book:

Cow Hampshire (blog). Cowhampshireblog.com.

Find a Grave. Findagrave.com.

Murder by Gaslight. Murderbygaslight.com.

New England Historical Society. Newenglandhistoricalsociety.com.

New Hampshire Old Graveyard Association. NHGraveyards.org.

Seacoast New Hampshire and South Coast Maine. SeacoastNH.com.

INDEX

V

Viell, Alfred 107

W

Wagner, Louis 44, 45, 46, 47, 48
Walford, Jane 115
Warren, Amory 109
Washington, New Hampshire 53,
     70
Watcher, the 63
Webster, Abel 67, 70
Webster, Daniel 62
Webster, Stephen 67, 70
Weight of Water, The 48
Wentworth, Benning 30, 31, 32, 88
White Island 40, 48
Williams, Minnie 19
World's Fair 18, 21

ABOUT THE AUTHOR

*R*enee Mallett is the author of *Haunted Colleges and Universities of Massachusetts* and many other books exploring the history, legends and lore of the New England states. She has published numerous pieces of writing ranging from short fiction to poetry and celebrity interviews to travel essays. Her fine art is showcased in galleries and private collections across New England and has been exhibited in Ireland and Italy as part of Carrara Marble Week.

Renee Mallett lives in southern New Hampshire with her family. Readers are invited to visit her in her studio at Western Avenue Studios, located at 122 Western Avenue in Lowell, Massachusetts, the first Saturday of each month for Open Studios. Or you can visit her on the web anytime at www. ReneeMallett.com.